AIRCRAFT PICTORIAL #8

F4U-1 CORSAIR

by Dana Bell

CLASSIC WARSHIPS PUBLISHING
P. O. Box 57591 • Tucson, AZ 85732 • USA
Web Site: www.classicwarships.com • Ph/Fx (520)748-2992

ISBN 978-0-9857149-9-4
Printed by Arizona Lithographers, Tucson, Arizona

General History of the Vought F4U-1 Corsair – Vol. 2

Our second look at the Vought-Brewster-Goodyear (VBG) Corsair family covers the raised cabin variants: the "-1A," -1C, and -1D. These most-widely produced Corsairs mastered the Pacific skies and developed into the Navy's and Marines' first single-seat fighter bombers. This technical history, based on two years' archival research, illustrates the story with photos that should be new to most readers. (A few favorite images appear, with new explanations, and some lesser-quality photos show features unseen in clearer images.) As always, I appreciate the help from the authors and researchers listed on page 72, though any errors are mine.

Project 108 – The Raised Cabin. Though superior to other US fighters, the Birdcage Corsair was not perfect. The greatest problem was the pilot's restricted view, blocked by the aircraft's nose (over 13 feet from eyeball to cowl lip) and obstructive canopy frames. At the direction of the Navy's Bureau of Aeronautics (BuAer), Vought began Engineering Project 108 to raise the pilot and improve his view, with kits planned to modify existing Birdcages. After the first Birdcage prototyped the raised cabin in February 1943, the Aircraft Armament Unit recommended halting Corsair production to speed the switch to the raised cabin – an unrealistic suggestion, with incomplete engineering drawings and the first revised aircraft months from completion. In April – three months before a revised prototype's delivery – BuAer ordered manufacture of the raised-cabin aircraft as soon as possible "without seriously affecting production." Delays securing vendor parts meant deliveries of the first "1943 Corsairs" would not begin until August.

The Birdcage Corsair's pilot seat allowed a six-inch vertical adjustment. In the raised-cockpit, a new frame placed the same seat inches farther forward at a more upright angle. The lowest position was identical in both cockpits, but the new mount could raise the seat nine inches. Controls and instruments were raised for pilot comfort, and the canopy was redesigned to increase headroom and eliminate most canopy frames. The gunsight reflector moved to the top of the windscreen frame, with revised armored glass positioned between the windscreen and the reflector. In June, the costs and time needed for these changes forced BuAer to cancel plans reconfiguring older Corsairs.

In February 1943, Vought sought to redesignate the Raised Cabin variant. Drawings could then be readily distinguished, and the unwieldy terms F4U-1 Raised Cabin Version, Raised Cockpit Version, 1943 Model Corsair, and Project 108 Corsair could be dropped. BuAer, however, rejected the request. Manufacturers were allowed to use the -1A suffix internally though, and the designation found its way into popular and official documents. BuAer was the final arbiter of designations, but Vought was correct that a redesignation would reduce confusion; this book will also use the -1A suffix.

External Stores – Centerline Racks. In December 1942, work began on an external 160-gallon centerline fuel tank; Vought began modifying a Birdcage Corsair to flight-test the tank and subcontracted for the tanks themselves. The tests began in mid-1943, by which time Brewster was also developing a bomb rack conversion. The tank and bomb rack were successful, but other, higher priorities delayed their introduction. An electrical bomb release actually entered production 69 aircraft before the first mounts were installed. For the British, Vought produced 86 retrofit kits to mount the tanks and racks on earlier Corsair Mark IIs (JT195 thru JT280).

Twin Pylons: the -1D. Even as the first centerline tanks entered production, BuAer asked for a new wing center section twin pylon configuration. A September 1943 memo specified provisions for a bomb on each pylon, or a drop tank on the right pylon only. By January 1944, flight tests were underway and the pylons soon entered production. In March 1944 the Navy decided that both pylons should carry fuel tanks; so-rigged, the aircraft were to be designated F4U-1D, FG-1D, and F3A-1D. Vought's first 290 twin-pylon Corsairs carried drop tank provisions on the right side only; they were designated F4U-1As until June, when BuAer decided all twin-pylon Corsairs would be called -1Ds, and also ordered drop tank provisions retrofitted to left-hand pylons. (All FG-1Ds carried tanks on both pylons, while Brewster's F3A-1Ds never entered production.)

Initially, -1Ds retained all provisions for centerline tanks and bomb racks. However, once the pylons had shown their worth, the centerline fuel provisions and electrical bomb arm/release capabilities were dropped. Subsequent aircraft retained the mounts, adding a manual bomb release at the pilot's left elbow. By early 1945 the centerline mounts were rewired with new electrical arming/dropping provisions, and new fuel lines were added. Since most 160-gallon centerline tanks had been expended as napalm bombs, the Brewster bomb racks were then adapted to carry standard 150-gallon fuel tanks.

20mm Cannons: the -1C. Any F4U-1 mounting four 20mm guns was designated as an F4U-1C. The first was a Birdcage, with remaining 200 aircraft converted from F4U-1Ds. By July 1945 squadrons were enthusiastic about the heavier weapons – VMF-314 asked only for two additional guns per aircraft and additional ammo! In September the CNO recommended standardizing the 20s for future fighter bombers. Oddly, for all the enthusiasm, 47 F4U-1Cs were modified back to-1Ds in early 1945.

Export Corsairs – Britain and New Zealand. Britain's Fleet Air Arm and the Royal New Zealand Air Force also flew Corsairs during WWII. RNZAF production was simple – the planes were identical to their American counterparts. When some New Zealand allocations were "borrowed" by US units, American deliveries were simply diverted to correct the error.

FAA deliveries were more complicated. Most British aircraft carried British radios and oxygen systems, as well as British camouflage and markings (using US paints).

FAA aircraft were the Corsair Mark I (Vought Birdcages), Mark II (F4U-1As and -1Ds), Mark IIIs (F3A-1As), and Mark IVs (FG-1As and -1Ds) – titles that did not apply to RNZAF Corsairs. (VBG often designated British Corsairs as -1Bs, another designation allowed but not approved by BuAer.)

Originally, the FAA Corsair was too tall for British hangar decks: with folded wings, the Corsair was 16 feet, 2.3 inches tall, while the hangars' transverse beams left only sixteen feet of clearance! The first 175 Corsair marks I and II and the first 73 Corsair IIIs were delivered with the taller US Navy wings, spanning 40 feet, 11-3/4 inches. Beginning in February 1944, many of these aircraft were refitted with fiberglass wingtips, shortening the span to about 40 feet, 1 inch. The tips were subsequently fitted during production.

In April 1944, BuAer learned FAA Corsairs were still too tall; the Royal Navy reported that newer carrier hangars were even shorter, and the new Corsair tail wheel raised the aircraft's height. Brewster then created a new "short short" fiberglass wingtip, which reduced the span to 39 feet, 9-1/2 inches. The short short tips were retrofitted to Corsair IIs and IIIs, but not to Corsair Is (by then used only for training). All Corsair IVs used the short short tips.

Corsair cockpits seemed to collect carbon monoxide. One source was the aft fuselage, where an aerodynamic fluke drew in exhaust gasses, pressurized them, and forced them forward past the radios and armor plate. The Navy preferred to reseal a bulkhead, but British engineers insisted on a simple vent system: a scoop on either side of the fuselage drew in fresh air, pushing fumes out through a ventral exhaust. The vents were introduced in Brewster production, installed on all Goodyear Mark IVs, and retrofitted by Britain to earlier aircraft.

Reconnaissance Corsairs. Despite attempts to develop the wartime Corsair into a recon fighter, structural and center-of-gravity issues were not easily solved. Plans to convert fifty Corsairs into F4U-1Ps died in early 1944. A number of Corsairs carried smaller cameras for strike photography, documenting ground attack missions. In August 1944, MCAS Cherry Point produced a mount adapting the Army K-25 camera for Marine squadrons, with sixty aircraft modified. (Photos of these aircraft give no clue as to how the cameras were installed.)

In early 1945, BuAer approved a lightweight San Diego camera installation, though records do not indicate if many Corsairs were modified. Several Marine units produced their own installations, notifying BuAer months after the designs had been in service. In January 1945, Commander Aircraft Pacific asked for camera installations in every command aircraft, though, again, no records show if or how any aircraft were modified.

Brewster Corsairs. Though Brewster Corsairs are often cited as inferior, Navy records do not agree. By January 1944, BuAer considered production of the first F3A-1Ds (beginning with BuNo 11467) or F3A-4s when the first Corsair III order finished. Brewster engineers had handled special projects, such as the shorter British wingtips, the centerline bomb rack, and a (poorly documented) high-lift Corsair wing. Brewster, however, had management and labor problems – raising the costs and delaying F3A deliveries. By early 1944, the Navy was pleased with Brewster production, but in April a new board of directors was elected. Unhappy with several of the members, the Navy terminated Brewster contracts 22 May, allowing completion of up to 150 more aircraft by 1 July. Lawsuits followed, and most of BuAer's Brewster files were pulled by legal offices – leaving little documentation in today's archives.

Goodyear Corsairs. Nearly a fourth of FG-1s (965 of 4,007 aircraft) were delivered as landplanes, with tail hooks deleted, wings locked, and extra weight removed (catapult hooks were retained for carrier deliveries). Folding wings returned when the Navy resumed Corsair carrier ops in late 1944. Production of Goodyear's planned FG-4 and F2G was delayed by the end of Brewster's contract, which moved British orders to Goodyear. Even with this disruption, the first FG-4s were nearing completion as the war ended.

Return to Carriers. In early tests, the Navy declared the Corsair an excellent carrier fighter. But those tests had been flown by highly experienced pilots, who also noted difficulties with cockpit visibility and a sudden vicious stall. By August 1943, the visibility problem had been solved by the raised cabin (at that time in full production) and the stall had been countered by the addition of a stall strip. VF-17 had qualified to operate from the new *Essex*-class carrier *USS Bunker Hill CV-17*, though skill was needed to manage a newly discovered landing bounce. Then, on 19 August 1943, the Commander Air Forces, Pacific Fleet, decided to simplify supply lines by approving Hellcats as the sole carrier fighter, moving Corsairs to island bases.

The landing bounce problem was solved by year's end, when Vought pressurized main oleo struts. Tests through spring 1944 showed the bounce had been completely eliminated, with landings smooth enough even for novice pilots. (VOF-1 found the Corsair 100% satisfactory, with the "finest anti-bounce properties of current types of carrier planes.") In January 1944, the Chief of Naval Operations asked ComAirPac to reconsider the logistical problems, and equip at least four air groups with Corsairs. BuAer supported the recommendation, noting that the F6F was "better suited to operations by extremely inexperienced personnel," but that the Corsair was "the better military ship as a day fighter." (Further, the new F4U-4 promised a 20-mph speed advantage over the F6F-5!)

Japan's introduction of the Kamikaze in October 1944 left the Navy scrambling to increase the number of carrier fighters. In the last week of 1944, Corsairs of VMF-124 and VMF-213 were finally assigned to the *USS Essex CV-9*, even though the Marine pilots had received minimal carrier and navigational experience. The squadron would lose more crews and aircraft to accidents than to enemy action.

The Navy increased Marine carrier training, and more Navy pilots transitioned into Corsairs. By V-J Day, seven Navy and fourteen Marine Corsair squadrons had fought from eleven carriers. After the war, carrier F6Fs would be replaced by newer Corsair models.

Canopies, Windscreens, and Sights. By September 1944, Vought had developed a new armored glass which doubled as a reflector – this was added to production lines and could be retrofitted to earlier aircraft. Postwar weight-saving orders deleted the armored glass on many Corsairs, forcing the return of the earlier reflector. (A flat windscreen, combining the armored glass, gunsight reflector, and windshield, was also tested and approved, but would not see production until the F4U-4.)

In 1944 the bubble canopy was successfully tested on two FG-1As; wartime installations were canceled to avoid any production interruptions. Vought introduced a single-piece "bubble canopy" in 1944. While offering improved vision and easy attachment to the production airframe, the canopy was not was we would today call a bubble and never saw production, but it did lead to a single piece canopy without horizontal crossbars. The simplified canopy entered production when the -1D and -1C variants were in production, though it was frequently retrofitted to earlier aircraft.

Engines and Accessories. With minor accessory improvements, the Pratt & Whitney R-2800-8 Double Wasp served the Corsair well. In the thinner air at high altitudes, the ignition system tended to arc, leading to engine failure. By January 1944 new aircraft were delivered with pressurized magnetos and distributors, and cast ignition harnesses – which were also shipped as kits for earlier aircraft. For greater emergency power, a water injection system was introduced in late 1943 (with a switch to the R-2800-8W engine). In mid-1944, Vought and Goodyear began delivering Corsairs with electric starters and a second battery. Kits were available to replace the cartridge starters on earlier aircraft, with the work frequently accomplished at Navy facilities in San Diego.

VBG delivered their early -1As with a eighteen fully operable cowl flaps; nearly all of these aircraft were field modified with fixed piece of aluminum sheet replacing the top three flaps. By late 1943, factories were installing a similar replacement part prior to delivery. In spring 1944 both types of "dead cowl flap skin" were reinforced to prevent them from being torn off in flight.

Integral Wing Fuel Tanks. To increase range, Vought designed a wet wing, sealing leading edges of the outer wing panels to act as fuel tanks, adding lines, vents, and filler caps. The tanks were not self-sealing, though a CO2 purging system helped prevent internal tank fires. After a month in combat, pilots complained that the tanks often leaked, spilled fuel when hit by gunfire, and often wouldn't pass fuel to the engine in flight. When possible, missions were flown with empty wing tanks, and in November 1943 units were authorized to remove the plumbing and CO2 system. In mid-1944, Vought and Goodyear eliminated the wing tanks in production.

Rocket Projectiles. In August 1944 BuAer approved the Mark 5 rocket system, with four 3.5-inch or 5-inch projectiles under each wing, for production installation; the launchers were also retrofitted to earlier aircraft. The first 152 F4U-1Cs were wired for rockets but delivered without the racks, while the last 48 were delivered with-out racks or wiring. The final 205 FG-1Ds were also wired for the 11.75-inch Tiny Tim rocket.

Pyrotechnics. In February 1944 VBG added an M5 flare pistol and downward-firing blast tube near the pilot's right thigh. BuAer soon discovered that when the first flare blasted away a doped fabric patch on the lower fuselage, carbon monoxide entered the cockpit. In May the pistol was ordered removed from the tube (to be fired only through the open cockpit), and the tube was ordered sealed with a wooden plug. Remaining Vought and Brewster -1s were delivered with plugged tubes, and later-production FG-1Ds deleted the tube altogether. In February 1945, Vought ordered the blast tubes removed from all Corsairs.

Radios and Antennas. Dash-1A Corsairs used the ATA/ARA command set with three MHF (medium-high frequency) receivers and two MHF transmitters. Shortages forced the occasional substitution of Army SCR-274N radios, as used on at least 82 FG-1As. Some Navy F4U-1As also carried a Western Electric WE-233A (ARC-4) VHF (very-high frequency) radio that, due to limited availability, was not issued to the Marines. In 1944, the ARC-5 command set began to replace the ATA/ARA, offering VHF ranges at the cost of some MHF channels. (Due to shortages, training units and the Atlantic Fleet were often still issued the ATA/ARA.) Needing more MHF channels, in mid-1944 the Navy instructed manufacturers replace the ARC-5's VHF components with additional MHF components, and to add a new, ten-channel ARC-1 VHF radio.

The MHF aerial was originally rigged from the forward mast to the rudder top and back to a right-side fuselage fitting behind the canopy. The 33.25-inch-tall phenolic plastic forward mast, which was prone to snapping off in flight, was soon replaced by a 32-inch aluminum sheet mast; when this also broke in flight, it was reduced to 24 inches, but breakage continued, and it was replaced by a heavier-gauge aluminum mast, also available in 32-inch and 24-inch lengths. Since none of these masts proved unbreakable, many operational Corsairs simply rigged the aerial to different points on the tail.

In early 1944, pilots noted MHF radio failures as they taxied or approached for landing. The problem was traced to the fully opened canopy shorting the antenna lead behind the cockpit. The solution was a semicircular notch cut into the trailing edge of the canopy frame. The notch became superfluous when a rearranged radio compartment moved the MHF sets to the left side of the fuselage; the antenna lead-in was also moved to the left side, well aft of the open canopy, in April 1945.

The field-installed VHF radio antennas were mounted inside a short dorsal AN74BX mast aft of the canopy; due to breakage, the mast was often replaced by a short whip antenna. The heavier replacement AN104AX mast also appeared on aircraft with factory-installed VHF sets.

The initial homing set was the ZB-3 (AN/ARR-1), with a retractable beaded-tipped, ventral wire antenna between stations 205-1/2 and 122-1/2. This was replaced by the ZB-X (ARR-2) – using the same antenna – beginning in early 1944; a fixed antenna mount was introduced in mid-1945.

A handful of early -1As used the ABD-1 or ABE-1 IFF (identification, friend or foe) system, distinguished by external wires between the stabilizer tips and fuselage sides. Others used the ABK-1, older ABF-1, or (after 1944) newer APX-1, all of which used a single, wire antenna just aft of the bombing window/ventral cockpit hatch.

Colors and Markings. The first raised cabin Corsairs were delivered in the graded, four-toned camouflages explained in Volume 1; the Blue Gray/Light Gray camouflage was never applied to a -1A or subsequent Corsair. Glossy Sea Blue camouflage was introduced at Vought and Goodyear in May 1944, with Brewster (at that time preparing to end production) followed soon after.

While RNZAF aircraft used US Navy colors, British Corsair IIs and IIIs used the scheme illustrated on pages 32 and 33. Unlike the US aircraft (which were painted with lacquers and dopes), these Corsairs were painted with enamels – eliminating color differences between fabric and metal surfaces. By the time Goodyear began producing Corsair IVs, Britain agreed to accept those aircraft in overall Glossy Sea Blue.

Corsair interior colors were changing as the first raised cockpit aircraft were introduced. The pink/orange "salmon" primer might have been found on some subcontracted components, such as outer wing panels, but it would quickly be replaced in production by one or two coats of yellow zinc chromate on most surfaces. Most cockpits were painted Interior Green (with a small number of F4U-1As wearing Vought's "candy-apple green" aluminized zinc chromate). However, well into 1944 Dull Dark Green continued to appear on subassemblies, as was found during the restoration of the National Air and Space Museum's F4U-1D (shown inside the back cover). In March 1945, Goodyear agreed to paint cockpits flat black above the side instrument consoles. Two months later, NAS Jacksonville reported that its reconditioning of older Corsairs included repainting all cockpits Interior Green, while in August 1946 MCAS Cherry Point reported refinishing its Corsair cockpits flat black with Glossy Sea Blue from two inches below the cockpit rails to the fuselage top.

One last note concerns landing gear colors. In February 1945, Goodyear noted the requirement that landing gear mechanisms were to be painted Glossy Sea Blue. Subcontractor Chrysler, however, still had a five-month supply of the Light Gray lacquer (then being used for landing gear) which would continue in use nearly through the end of the war. Cherry Point again used its own postwar variation, refinishing main gear legs in Interior Green while painting tail gear Glossy Sea Blue.

SERIALS

(Serials are shown in construction order with construction sequence numbers in parentheses; note that many BuAer serial numbers were assigned out of order)

VOUGHT SERIAL RANGES

Serials	Type
(0950) 17647 – (0999) 17696	F4U-1A
(1000) 17697/JT195 – (1024) 17721/JT219	Corsair II
(1025) 17722 – (1054) 17751	F4U-1A
(1055) 17752/JT220 – (1079) 17776/JT244	Corsair II
(1080) 17777 – (1149) 17846	F4U-1A
(1150) 17847/JT245 – (1174) 17871/JT269	Corsair II
(1175) 17872 – (1254) 17951	F4U-1A
(1255) 17952/JT270 – (1265) 17962/JT280	Corsair II
(1266) 17963 – (1384) 18081	F4U-1A
(1385) 18082/JT281 – (1409) 18106/JT305	Corsair II
(1410) 18107 – (1424) 18121	F4U-1A
(1425) 55784 – 1479) 55838	F4U-1A
(1480) 55839/JT306 – (1504) 55863/JT330	Corsair II
(1505) 55864 – (1584) 55943	F4U-1A
(1585) 55944/JT331 – (1609) 55968/JT355	Corsair II
(1610) 55969 – (1689) 56048	F4U-1A
(1690) 56049/JT356 – (1714) 56073/JT380	Corsair II
(1715) 56074 – (1804) 56163	F4U-1A
(1805) 56164/JT381 – (1829) 56188/JT405	Corsair II
(1830) 56189 – (1919) 56278	F4U-1A
(1920) 56279/JT406 – (1938) 56297/JT424	Corsair II
(1939) 56298 – (2124) 56483	F4U-1A

Serials	Type
(2125) 49660 – (2544) 50079	F4U-1A
(2545) 50080/JT425 – (2614) 50149/JT494	Corsair II
(2615) 50150 – (2694) 50229	F4U-1A
(2695) 50230/JT495 – (2729) 50264/JT529	Corsair II
(2730) 50265 – (2789) 50324	F4U-1A
(2790) 50325/JT530 – (2814) 50349/JT554	Corsair II
(2815) 50350/JT555 – (2824) 50359/JT564	-1D/Mk.II
(2825) 50360 – (2924) 50459	F4U-1D
(2925) 50460/JT565 – (2959) 50494/JT599	Corsair II
(2960) 50495 – (3039) 50574	F4U-1D
(3040) 50575/JT600 – (3074) 50609/JT634	Corsair II
(3075) 50610 – (3124) 50659	F4U-1D
(3125) 57084 – (3149) 57108	F4U-1D
(3150) 57109/JT635 – (3184) 57143/JT669	Corsair II
(3185) 57144 – (3255) 57214	F4U-1D
(3256) 57215/JT670 – (3290) 57249/JT704	Corsair II
(3291) 57250 – (3607) 57566	F4U-1D
(3608) 57567 – (3610) 57569	F4U-1C
(3611) 57570 – (3817) 57776	F4U-1D
(3818) 57777 – (3832) 57791	F4U-1C
(3833) 57792 – (4006) 57965	F4U-1D
(4007) 57966 – (4024) 57983	F4U-1C
(4025) 82178 – (4036) 82189	F4U-1C

Serials	Type
(4037) 82190 – (4106) 82259	F4U-1D
(4107) 82260 – (4136) 82289	F4U-1C
(4137) 82290 – (4216) 82369	F4U-1D
(4217) 82370 – (4241) 82394	F4U-1C
(4242) 82395 – (4281) 82434	F4U-1D
(4282) 82435 – (4306) 82459	F4U-1C
(4307) 82460 – (4386) 82539	F4U-1D
(4387) 82540 – (4429) 82582	F4U-1C
(4430) 82583 – (4479) 82632	F4U-1D
(4480) 82633 – (4486) 82639	F4U-1C
(4487) 82640 – (4586) 82739	F4U-1D
(4587) 82740 – (4608) 82761	F4U-1C
(4609) 82762 – (4699) 82852	F4U-1D

F4U-1A FACTORY CHANGES

(0950) 17647 – introduce raised cabin, headrest, canopy armor.
(0953) 17650 – introduce modified arresting hook head.
(1233) 17930 – introduce stall warning, combined landing gear/dive brake handle, rudder trough superstructure, 32-inch aluminum mast.
(1234) 17931 – introduce CL electrical bomb arm/release.
(1302) 17999 – introduce CL tank/bomb mounts.
(1411) 18108 – test twin center section shackles.

(1551) 55910 – introduce water injection.
(1552) 55911 – introduce pressurized ignition.
(1825) JT401 – introduce 24-inch aluminum mast.
(2053) 56412 – test rocket projectiles.
(2073) 56432 – introduce VHF mast.
(2103) 56462 – delete landing light.
(2129) 49664 – modified to XF4U-3B.
(2225) 49760 – introduce ARC-5 radio; ZB-X (ARR-2).
(2275) 49810 – introduce forged tail wheel yoke, half-round canopy release.
(2325) 49860 – introduce dead cowl flap.
(2425) 49960 – delete oil tank armor.
(2447) 49982 – introduce APX-1 instead of ABK.
(2505) 50040 – introduce M8 flare pistol.
(2512) 50047 – delete bulkhead 134 armor plate.
(2531) 50066 – delete bombing window.
(2545) JT425 – introduce short wingtips.

F4U-1C/F4U-1D FACTORY CHANGES
(2815) JT555 – delete wing fuel tanks; introduce twin pylons.
(3025) 50560 – introduce oleo strut dampening provisions.
(3105) 50640 – introduce left pylon fuel tank provisions.
(3124) 50659 – delete center section filler and surfacing.
(3125) 57084 – introduce Glossy Sea Blue finish, antenna cutout in canopy trailing edge, delete CL fuel tank lines.
(3225) 57184 – introduce ABA-1 radio provisions.
(3275) JT689 – delete M8 flare pistol blast tube.
(3286) JT700 – introduce half-round canopy release.
(3325) 57284 – delete tail wheel/arresting gear interconnecting control, introduce single piece canopy glass.
(3397) 57356 – introduce combat type prop.
(3425) 57384 – introduce additional trainer overturn structure.
(3524) 57483 – introduce left side windshield hand grip.
(3525) 57484 – introduce removable wing tip, electric starter.
(3625) 57584 – introduce bullet-proof windshield/reflector.
(3685) 57644 – delete stall warning.
(3822) 57781 – delete upward recognition light.
(3845) 57804 – introduce canopy trailing edge notch.
(3907) 57866 – introduce revised tail wheel door.
(3920) 57879 – introduce left arm and under-seat armor.
(4022) 57981 – introduce new right side fuselage hand grip.
(4100) 82253 – introduce rocket projectile mounts.
(4347) 82500 – introduce rocket-blast reinforced outer flaps.
(4374) 82527 – introduce flap step.

BREWSTER SERIAL RANGES

(0061) 04575 – (0174) 04688	F3A-1A
(0175) 04689/JS469 – (0260) 04774/JS554	Corsair III
(0261) 08550/JS555 – (0508) 08797/JS802	Corsair III
(0509) 11067/JS803 – (0594) 11152/JS888	Corsair III
(0595) 11153/JT963 – (0604) 11162/JT972	Corsair III
(0605) 11163 – (0735) 11293	F3A-1A

F3A-1A FACTORY CHANGES
(0061) 04575 – introduce raised cabin, CL tank/bomb mounts, canopy armor.
(0138) 04652 – introduce dead cowl flap.
(0147) 04661 – introduce CL electrical bomb arm/release.
(0159) 04673 – introduce 32-inch aluminum mast.
(0249) JS543 – introduce short wingtips.
(0261) JS555 – introduce stall warning.
(0263) JS557 – introduce half-round canopy release.
(0351) JS645 – introduce ARC-5 radio; ZB-X (ARR-2).
(0360) JS654 – introduce M-8 pyrotechnic pistol.
(0378) JS672 – introduce 24-inch aluminum mast.
(0605) 11163 – introduce ARC-1 VHF radio.
(0650) 11208 – introduce water injection.

GOODYEAR SERIAL RANGES

(0300) 13291 – (0479) 13470	FG-1A
(0480) 13471 – (0481) 13472	XF2G-1
(0482) 13473 – (1600) 14591	FG-1A
(1601) 14592/KD161 – (1699) 14690/KD259	Corsair IV
(1700) 14691 – (1704) 14695	XF2G
(1705) 14696/KD265 – (2000) 14991/KD560	Corsair IV
(2001) 76139/KD561	Corsair IV
(2002) 76140/KD562 – (2307) 76445/KD867	1D/Mk IV
(2308) 76446 – (2601) 76739	FG-1D
(2602) 87788 – (2762) 87948	FG-1D
(2763) 87949/KD868 – (2812) 87998/KD917	Corsair IV
(2813) 87999 – (2947) 88133	FG-1D
(2948) 88134/KD918 – (2972) 88158/KD942	Corsair IV
(2973) 88159 – (3082) 88268	FG-1D
(3083) 88269/KD943 – (3107) 88293/KD967	Corsair IV
(3108) 88294 – (3217) 88403	FG-1D
(3218) 88404/KD968 – (3242) 88428/KD992	Corsair IV
(3243) 88429 – (3267) 88453	FG-1D
(3268) 92007 – (3431) 92170	FG-1D
(3432) 92171/KD993 – (3438) 92177/KD999	Corsair IV
(3439) 92178/KE100 – (3456) 92195/KE117	Corsair IV
(3457) 92196 – (3962) 92701	FG-1D
(3963) 67055 – (4007) 67099	FG-1D

FG-1A FACTORY CHANGES
(0300) 13291 – introduce raised cabin.
(0301) 13292 – introduce CL rack provisions, half-round canopy release.
(0320) 13311 – introduce 32-inch aluminum mast.
(0328) 13319 – introduce welded tail wheel extension.
(0383) 13374 – test F2G-1 induction system and scoop.
(0401) 13392 – introduce stall warning.
(0426) 13417 – introduce dead cowl flap.
(0445) 13436 – introduce pressurized ignition.
(0480/1) 13471/2 – deliver as XF2G-1.
(0581) 13572 – introduce CL electrical bomb arm/release.
(0592) 13583 – introduce enlarged tail wheel door cutout.
(0636) 13627 – introduced fixed wing land-based version.
(0656) 13647 – introduce forged tail wheel yoke.
(0713) 13704 – dive test aircraft.
(0750) 13741 – introduce ARC-5 radio.
(0751) 13742 – introduce ZB-X (ARR-2).
(0800) 13791 – delete oil tank armor.
(0801) 13792 – introduce 24-inch aluminum mast.
(0901) 13892 – delete bombing window.
(1001) 13992 – introduce water injection, rudder trough superstructure.
(1100/01) 14091/92 – test bubble canopy.
(1221) 14212 – delete bulkhead 134 armor.
(1288) 14279 – introduce Glossy Sea Blue camouflage.
(1386) 14377 – introduce M-8 pyrotechnic pistol.
(1426) 14417 – introduce cutout in rear edge of canopy.
(1600) 14591 – end production of land-based Corsair.
(1601) KD161 – introduce British short short wingtip.
(1651) KD211 – introduce revised tail wheel door cutouts.
(1666) KD226 – introduce electric starter.
(1700-1704) 14691-14695 – divert to XF2G program.
(1751) KD311 – introduce tail wheel drag fairing.

FG-1D FACTORY CHANGES
(2002) KD562 – introduce armored glass reflector, left side windshield hand grip; delete landing light.
(2003) KD563 – delete stall warning.
(2011) KD571 – introduce combat prop; delete wing tanks.
(2102) KD662 – introduce frameless canopy.
(2201) KD761 – introduce left arm and under-seat armor.
(2202) KD762 – introduce fuselage right side hand grip.
(2273) KD833 – introduce rocket projectile mounts.
(2308) 76446 – introduce removable plastic wingtip.
(2309) 76447 – introduce ARC-1 VHF radio.
(2680) 87866 – delete M8 flare pistol blast tube.
(2686) 87872 – introduce flap step.
(3014) 88200 – delete non-skid wingwalk.
(3134) 88320 – introduce flat black cockpit above consoles.
(3302) 92041 – move MHF antenna lead to left side.
(3600) 92339 – introduce Grizzly 8-1/2 x 4 solid tail wheel.
(3602) 92341 – introduce aft fuselage carbon monoxide scoops.
(3802) 92541 – introduce 11.75-inch rocket installation.

BuNo 02557, the 405th F4U-1 built, tested the production modifications that would identify the "raised cabin" Corsair or F4U-1A. Serving with several units following flight tests, she eventually crashed near Atlantic City, New Jersey, on 28 January 1945 while assigned to VBF-92.

A production-model F4U-1A, BuNo 55901, assigned to VMF-222 on Bougainville in 1944.

Vought built 510 Corsair Mark IIs for Britain's Fleet Air Arm (360 based on the F4U-1A and 150 based on the -1D); Brewster built 430 Corsair IIIs (all based on the F3A-1A); and Goodyear built 852 Corsair Mark IVs (396 based on the FG-1A and 456 on the -1D). This FAA 1836 Squadron Corsair II (serial unknown) from *HMS Victorious* landed aboard *USS Essex CV-9* following strikes on Japan, 9 August 1945. Note the artwork on the right side of the engine cowl.

Vought fitted 20mm cannon wings to one F4U-1 (Birdcage) and 200 F4U-1Ds; all were redesignated F4U-1Cs. Although Marine units found the aircraft highly effective against aerial and ground targets, 47 aircraft were back-modified to F4U-1Ds in early 1945. This -1C was assigned to VMF-311 on Okinawa in mid-1945. The serial is unknown – no F4U-1C serials ended in "310."

The "-1D" suffix designated Corsairs equipped to carry two pylons beneath the wing center section. This F4U-1D, BuNo 50360, was the Navy's first production example; she was tested at NAS Patuxent River, Maryland, from July through September 1944.

The installation of an R-2800-14 engine and turbo supercharger converted several Corsairs to "-3" variants. The Naval Aircraft Modification Unit (NAMU) at Johnsville, Pennsylvania, was tasked to convert 27 FG-1Ds to FG-3s in 1946, though records do not confirm the number of aircraft actually modified. BuNo 92382, which crashed just south of Salem, Maryland, on 17 March 1948, was scheduled to make an attempt on the world altitude record of 56,460 feet.

A skillful crash landing minimized damage to the aircraft, but details of the ventral supercharger intake are unfortunately buried in the mud beneath the aircraft.

Seven Goodyear Corsairs were drawn from the production line for completion as F2Gs, perhaps the most beautiful aircraft of the entire family. BuNo 14692, seen here at Pax River on 1 November 1945, was configured for land-based operations as an XF2G-1. (Carrier-based variants were designated F2G-2.) With the closure of Brewster in mid-1944, Goodyear was forced to extend production of the FG-1D, dooming plans to produce the F2G (and FG-4) before the war's end.

(Left) The original Corsair prop blades were the 13'4" Hamilton Standard 6443A-21 on the F4U and the nearly identical 6526A-21 on the F3A and FG. (Right) The 13'1" "combat type" prop was introduced in late 1943. Featuring a much thicker chord near the hub, the blade was to be retrofitted to earlier aircraft when available, entering production at Vought on F4U-1D BuNo 57356 and at Goodyear with FG-1D BuNo 76149. The combat type props used two similar Hamilton Standard blade types: 6501A-0 or 6541A-0. All four blades were mounted in 23E50 hubs.

When Corsair ignitions began to arc at higher altitudes, BuAer ordered the magnetos, distributors, and ignition harnesses pressurized (simulating altitudes 10,000 feet lower).

These images show the pressurized distributors (to either side of the vertical prop blade) and the cast ignition harness on F4U-1Ds BuNo 50030 in August 1944 (left) and BuNo 50571 in July 1944 (above).

The earlier unpressurized system is illustrated on page 44.

(Left) The engine accessory bay on FG-1D BuNo 76657, photographed in 1948, shows the large oil tank without forward armor plate (deleted during production). Although the aircraft was delivered with tanks for the water injection system, these were removed after the war. Note the antenna mast, formed from sheet aluminum.

(Above) A closeup view of the oil tank, mounted on the firewall.

More than seven decades later, the R-2800-8W is still an impressive power plant. The engine's "W" suffix noted a water injection system, which included the tank seen atop the forward end of the accessory bay. FG-1D BuNo 14358 was one of three Corsairs involved in a 1944 attempt on the transcontinental speed record.

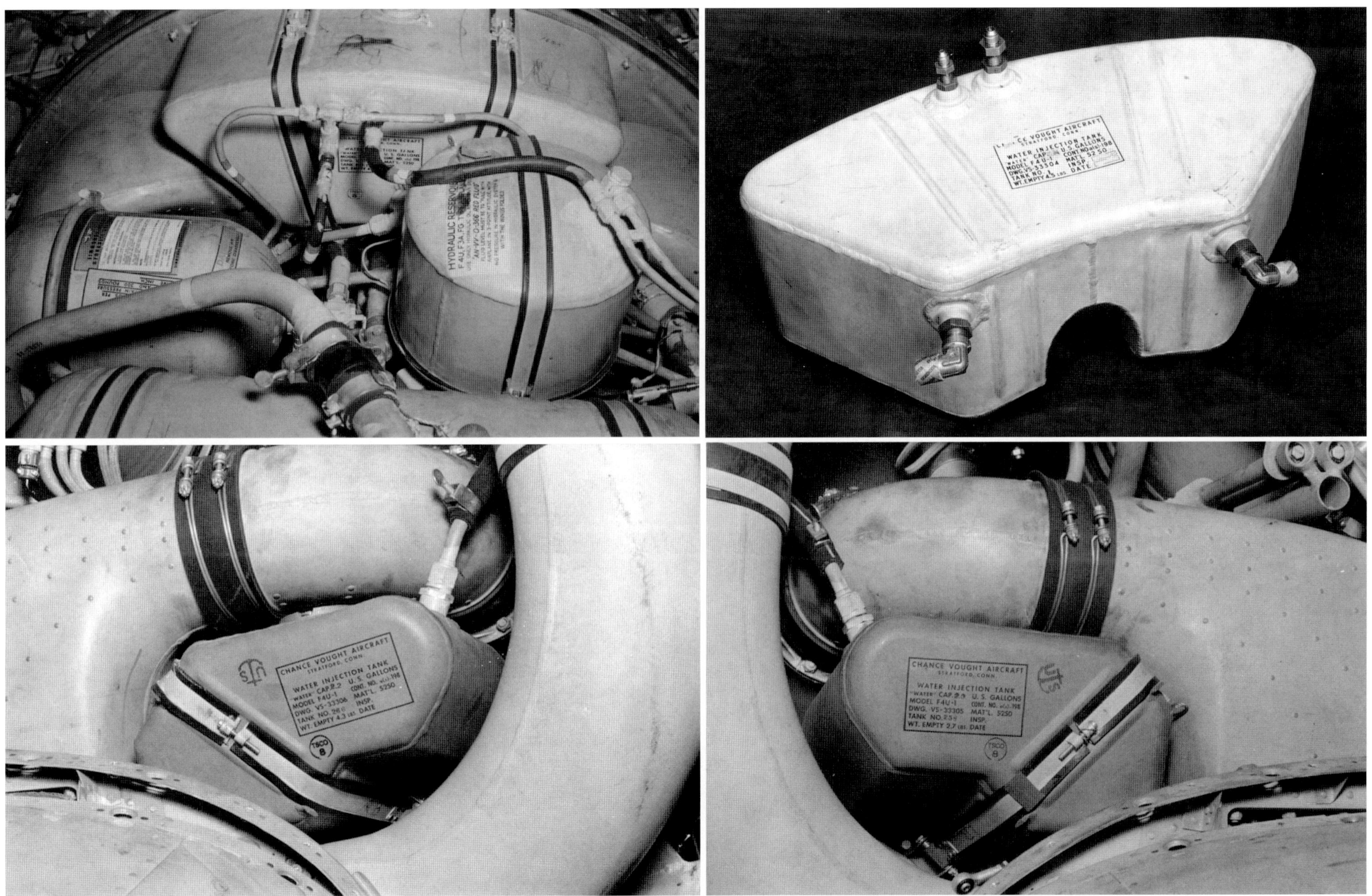

A water injection system was introduced during -1A production by all three Corsair manufacturers. Three welded-aluminum tanks – a 5.9-gallon main tank (top), 2.1-gallon right-side tank (left), and 2.3-gallon left-side tank (right) – held a water-alcohol mixture formulated to prevent freezing at altitude. Fully opening the throttle triggered a switch that pumped the mixture through the carburetor into the cylinders.

(Top right) Corsair fuselages frequently wrinkled following hard landings, a problem partially mitigated by a series of internal braces. (Top left) By 1945, many field organizations were adding an exterior sheet of aluminum alloy to strengthen the forward fuselage; this drawing was prepared on Guam in May 1945. (Main image) On 27 March 1948, FG-1D BuNo 88346 nosed over at NAS St Louis. The aircraft, which suffered minimal damage, clearly shows a reinforcement panel riveted to the fuselage side.

(Left) With the raised cockpit, the -1A Corsair needed a higher clearance for the pilot's head; Vought took the engineering opportunity to design a simpler canopy with fewer obstructions to the pilot's vision. The original greenhouse was replaced by three pieces of blown plexiglass, two horizontal support frames, and a removable, cast aluminum armor behind the pilot's head. (Center) A flat release button was soon added to the canopy's right side, allowing the ground crew quick access to the cockpit. (Right) the release mechanism (inset) was eventually enhanced with a half-round button for quicker access.

Impressed with the new canopy on the Army's P-47K (as bubble-topped P-47Ds were briefly known), BuAer asked Goodyear to develop a similar system for the Corsair in January 1944. The first of two aircraft (BuNo 14091, above) actually used a Thunderbolt canopy and windscreen. With a cut-down aft fuselage, the aircraft was retained by Goodyear for flight tests. The second aircraft (BuNo 14092, opposite page) was completed in May with Goodyear's own design for a "free-blown" canopy. Tested extensively by Goodyear and the Navy, in January 1945 the new fuselage and canopy were approved for use in the F2G. The forecast of production delays caused BuAer to drop plans for the new canopy on the FG-1Ds and F4U-4s. BuAer records show that 14092 subsequently tested a dorsal fin extension, "Brewster wings" (perhaps a variation of Brewster's elusive high-lift Corsair wings), and a Focke Wulf style antenna system (passing the antenna through the back of the canopy).

(Above) VMF-451 pilots complained that the new reflector was mounted too high, so their ground crews devised this simple modification. While not universally adopted, it would occasionally turn up on other operational Corsairs.

(Right) With the seat raised, the standard reflector for the Mark 8 gunsight was mounted too low for combat. A new reflector, mounted at the top of the windscreen, was fitted to all -1As to rectify the problem. (The unusual arrangement of the oxygen equipment in this September 1944 photo was a local modification designed by VMF-314.)

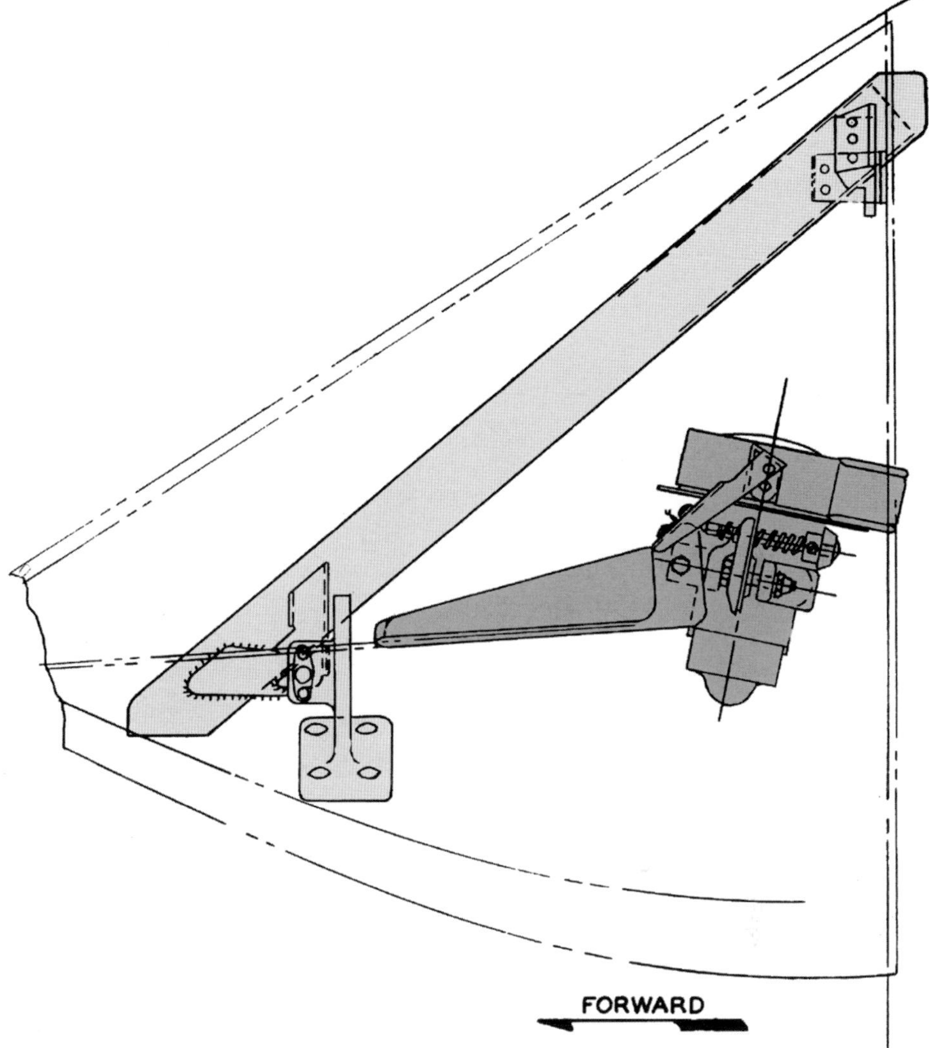

Simplification of the sighting system began in early 1944 with a design combining the bullet-proof glass and reflector and mounting the sight higher on the cockpit coaming. The new sight would be retrofitted to earlier aircraft beginning in late-1944, appearing on new FG-1Ds about the same time.

(Left) FG-1D BuNo 76508, which crashed on its January 1945 delivery flight, shows the simplified sighting system.

In May 1944, Vought delivered a new "bubble canopy" for Pax River's evaluation on F4U-1A BuNo 18051. Pilots reported improved visibility to the rear and quarters, though the plex gave some distortion and starry night reflections. Production of the new canopy was recommended, but delayed pending trials on Goodyear's "free blown" canopy. (See page 20)

Though a revised, frameless blown canopy didn't appear in production until late-August 1944, it was easily retrofitted to earlier aircraft once suppliers caught up. The new canopy's simpler cross-section offered poorer visibility than Vought's earlier design, but reduced drag and production costs. The aircraft above (F4U-1D BuNo 57608) also tested a flat windscreen that incorporated the armored glass and a gunsight reticle. Although approved for production in December 1944, the new windscreen wouldn't be introduced until the F4U-4. F4U-1D BuNo 57879 (right) crashed on a September 1944 delivery flight. Note the reintroduction of the emergency release button, which had been omitted from earlier frameless canopies. Note also the semi-circular cutout at the rear of the canopy frame – added to prevent the open canopy from shorting the MHF antenna wire.

(Above) The canopy interior framework was rigged with mirrors, locks, and releases. The seal beneath the headrest notes that this aircraft had been purchased by students from Danbury, Connecticut.

(Right) Crew chiefs had little room to help their pilots strap in before a mission. This VMF-211 chief found a workable solution on Bougainville in February 1944.

(Below) To keep seat straps from slipping off pilots' shoulders, a simple bracket was added to seat backs beginning in October 1944.

(Above left) Photographed in April 1944, F4U-1A BuNo 55794 displays a revised arrangement of controls for the new ARC-5 radio. Perhaps more interesting, the photo shows how the pilot's armor back plate hinged forward to act as a work surface for crews accessing the radios.

(Above right) With the increase in ground attack missions, most Corsairs were retrofitted with underseat armor; factory installations began with F4U BuNo 57879 and FG BuNo 76339.

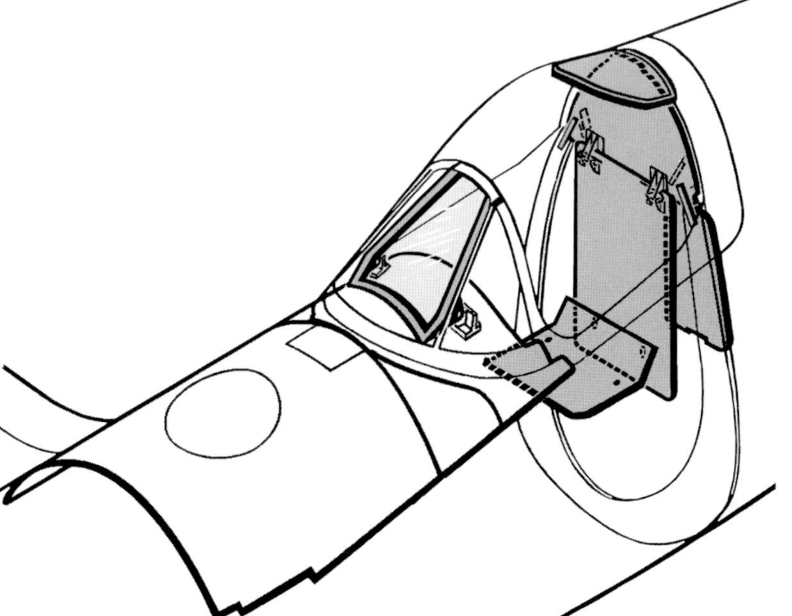

(Left) The quality (and weight) of pilot armor generally increased during Corsair production; some armor was also removed. The forward plate protecting the oil tank disappeared from production with F4U BuNo 49960 and FG BuNo 13791 and was deleted from earlier aircraft in the field. A similar plate forward of the windscreen (at Bulkhead 134) was deleted from FGs beginning with BuNo 14212, and retroactively removed from earlier Corsairs. The left side armor plate (protecting the pilot's throttle arm) was added in production at the same time as the underseat armor.

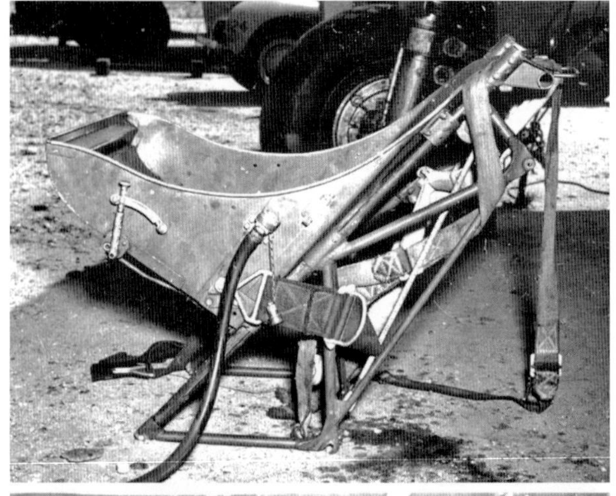

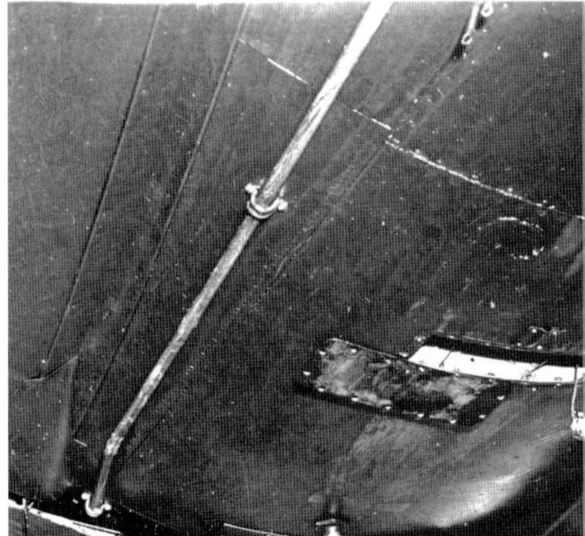

(Top) With the introduction of the G-suit in 1945, a pressure hose was added to the seat's left side.

(Above) Running the G-suit's pressure hose from the engine through the firewall was not a safe option, so the hose was run along the bottom of the fuselage up through the cockpit to the seat.

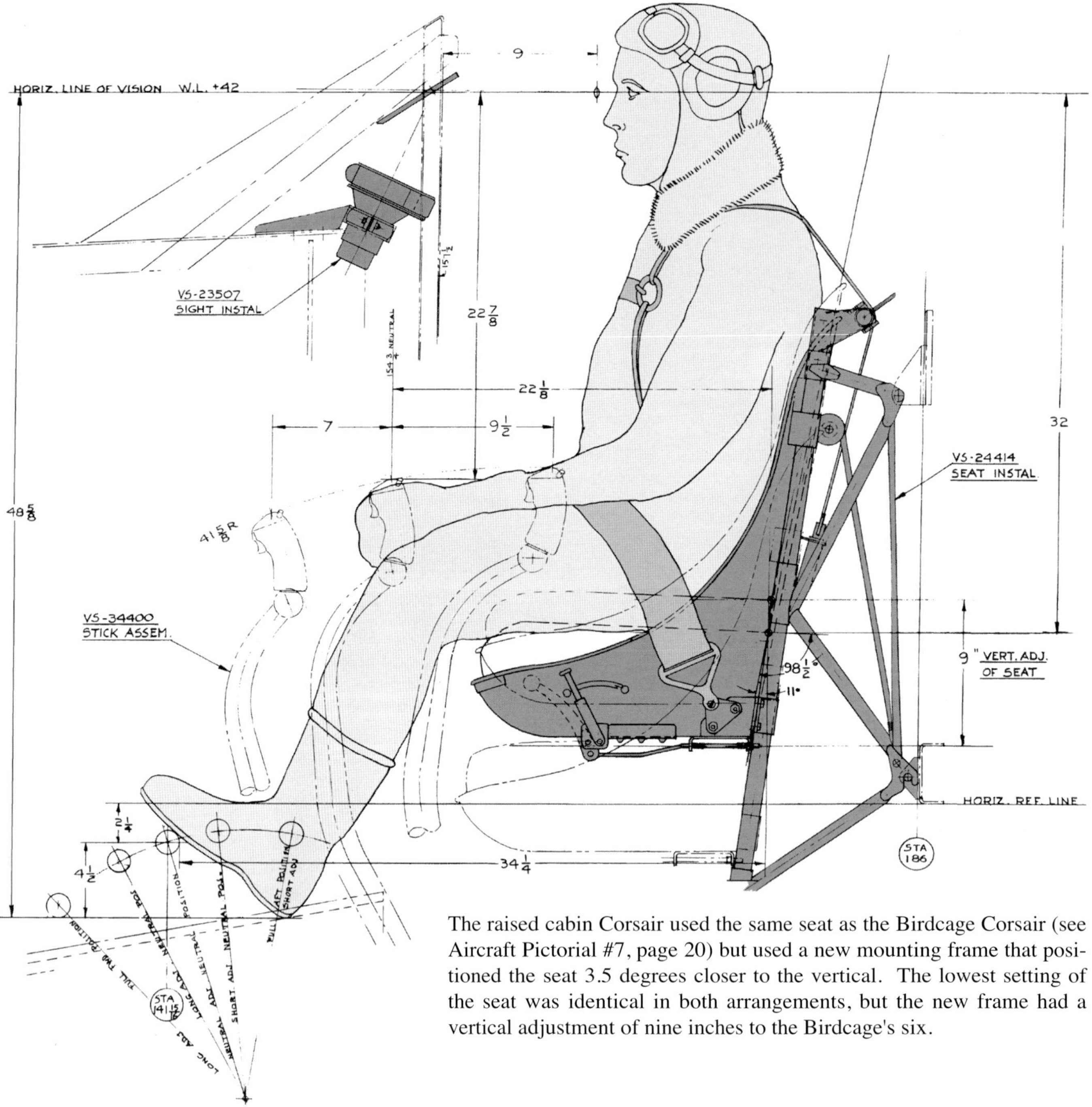
HORIZ. LINE OF VISION W.L. +42
9
VS-23507
SIGHT INSTAL
22 7/8
22 1/8
7
9 1/2
32
VS-24414
SEAT INSTAL
48 5/8
VS-34400
STICK ASSEM.
9" VERT. ADJ. OF SEAT
98 1/2°
11°
HORIZ. REF. LINE
2 1/4
4 1/2
34 1/4
STA 186

The raised cabin Corsair used the same seat as the Birdcage Corsair (see Aircraft Pictorial #7, page 20) but used a new mounting frame that positioned the seat 3.5 degrees closer to the vertical. The lowest setting of the seat was identical in both arrangements, but the new frame had a vertical adjustment of nine inches to the Birdcage's six.

A British maintenance crew works on a Corsair Mark II at an American training base.

Each revised radio installation brought a change in the radio controls to the pilot's right side. The most common Corsair mount was the ATA-ARA, as seen here in May 1945. Seen from the left, the boxes above the side console represent the ZB homing set (below a spherical black knob that extended the ZB antenna when pulled aft); a junction box (below a positionable light fixture); three ARA receiver controls; the ATA transmitter control; and (cropped by the photographer) the IIF control/destruction box.

The left side of the cockpit from BuNo 17930, an early F4U-1A photographed in December 1943. Although the consoles and controls are mounted slightly higher for pilot comfort, few things have changed from a similar view of the Birdcage Corsair. This was the first Corsair to use the new "gearshift" type lever, covered in detail on page 34. Inside the canopy rail is the fourteen-inch rack lock with five stops; on later aircraft this would be shortened to five inches, cutting of the forward three stops.

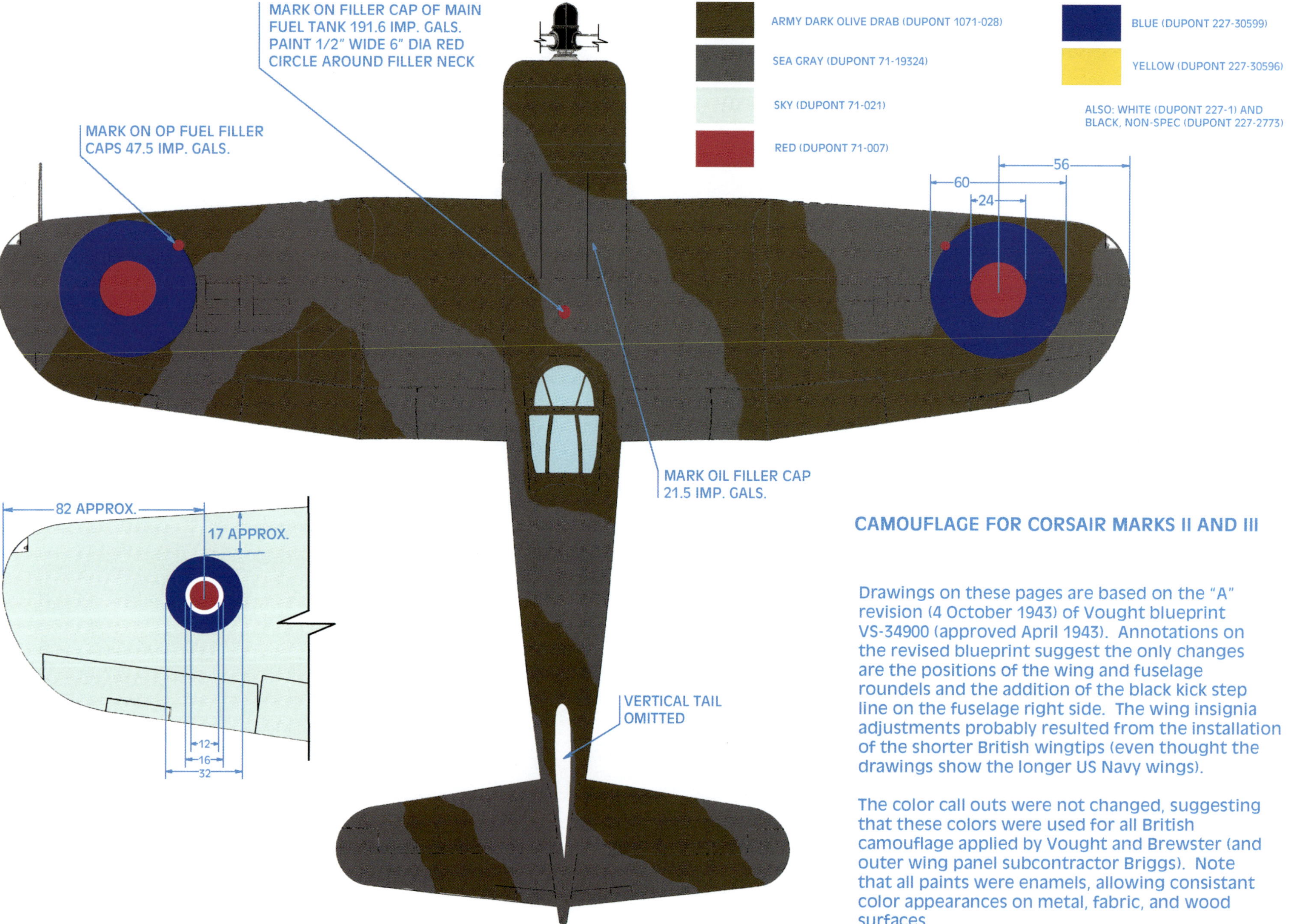

CAMOUFLAGE FOR CORSAIR MARKS II AND III

Drawings on these pages are based on the "A" revision (4 October 1943) of Vought blueprint VS-34900 (approved April 1943). Annotations on the revised blueprint suggest the only changes are the positions of the wing and fuselage roundels and the addition of the black kick step line on the fuselage right side. The wing insignia adjustments probably resulted from the installation of the shorter British wingtips (even thought the drawings show the longer US Navy wings).

The color call outs were not changed, suggesting that these colors were used for all British camouflage applied by Vought and Brewster (and outer wing panel subcontractor Briggs). Note that all paints were enamels, allowing consistant color appearances on metal, fabric, and wood surfaces

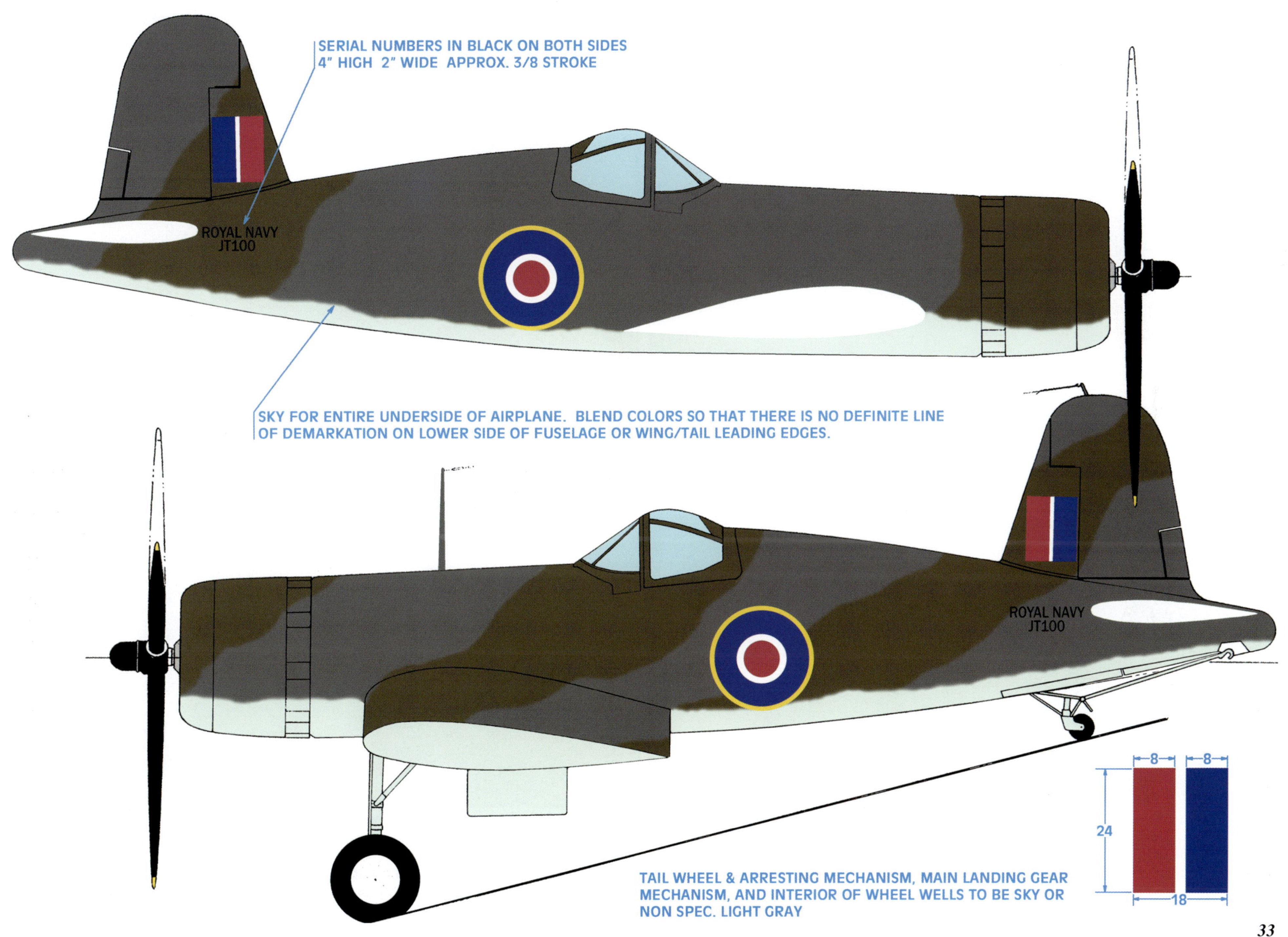
SERIAL NUMBERS IN BLACK ON BOTH SIDES
4" HIGH 2" WIDE APPROX. 3/8 STROKE
ROYAL NAVY
JT100
SKY FOR ENTIRE UNDERSIDE OF AIRPLANE. BLEND COLORS SO THAT THERE IS NO DEFINITE LINE
OF DEMARKATION ON LOWER SIDE OF FUSELAGE OR WING/TAIL LEADING EDGES.
ROYAL NAVY
JT100
8
8
24
18
TAIL WHEEL & ARRESTING MECHANISM, MAIN LANDING GEAR
MECHANISM, AND INTERIOR OF WHEEL WELLS TO BE SKY OR
NON SPEC. LIGHT GRAY

(Top left) When several pilots kicked the landing gear retraction control while taxiing, BuAer ordered a metal clip installed to prevent further accidents. To the left of the control is the gear position indicator and the dive brake control, which lowered the main gear to slow the aircraft in a dive.

(Top right) Beginning with F4U-1A BuNo 17930, the landing gear and dive brake levers were combined into a single unit to the left of the pilot's thigh. Moving the lever through the left channel operated the landing gear; the right channel operated the main gear as a dive brake. After the war, the right channel was often plated over to prevent the use of dive brakes. (Bottom left) The raised cabin moved the rudder pedals about a half an inch higher, with the pivot point moved slightly aft; the foot troughs were not moved at all, causing pilots to push the pedals down rather than fore-and-aft. The initial solution was to mount a wooden trough atop the original installation; this was superceded by a formed aluminum superstructure, as seen here, introduced on production lines with F4U BuNo 17930, FG BuNo 13992, and all F3A-1As. (Bottom right) Vought introduced this new oxygen regulator on BuNo 17818. To avoid drawing carbon monoxide into the regulator, a semi-circular ventilation ring was mounted over the system.

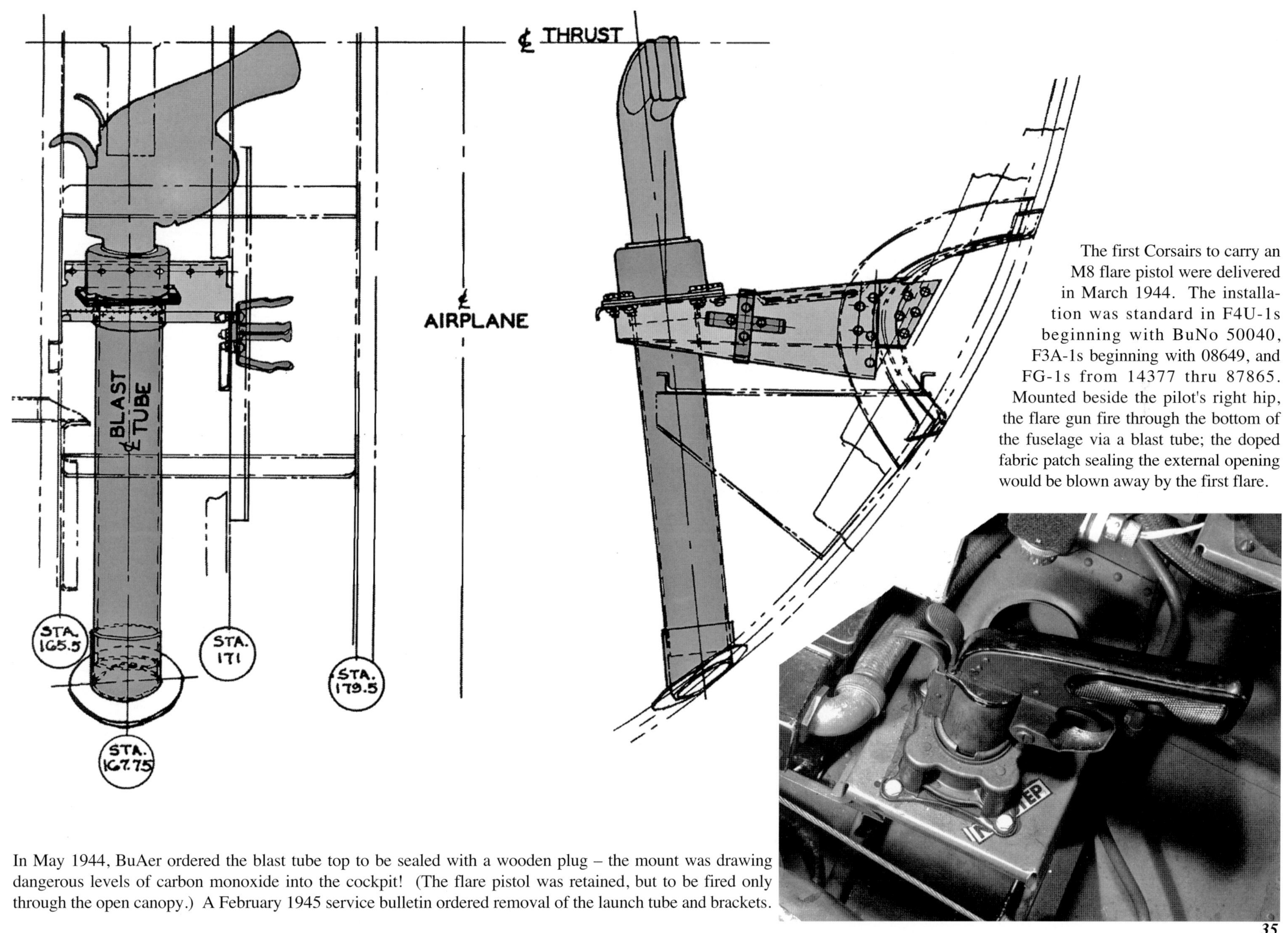

The first Corsairs to carry an M8 flare pistol were delivered in March 1944. The installation was standard in F4U-1s beginning with BuNo 50040, F3A-1s beginning with 08649, and FG-1s from 14377 thru 87865. Mounted beside the pilot's right hip, the flare gun fire through the bottom of the fuselage via a blast tube; the doped fabric patch sealing the external opening would be blown away by the first flare.

In May 1944, BuAer ordered the blast tube top to be sealed with a wooden plug – the mount was drawing dangerous levels of carbon monoxide into the cockpit! (The flare pistol was retained, but to be fired only through the open canopy.) A February 1945 service bulletin ordered removal of the launch tube and brackets.

The Service Squadron 14 (MAG-14) repair line on Green Island, May 1944. Note the lack of green primer on exposed areas of the Corsairs; beginning in late-summer 1943, Vought, Brewster, and Goodyear used one or two coats of untinted yellow zinc chromate primer for corrosion control.

Flying out of Lagoon Fighter Strip, Green Island, Lt. Lesley V. Strandtman's F4U-1A (BuNo 56194) was hit by anti-aircraft fire over Kavieng on 9 April 1944. The 40mm round passed through the right wing root, shattering the canopy, puncturing a tire, removing the aerial, and lacerating Strandtman's neck. The VMF-114 pilot brought his aircraft home, but crashed on landing. The remains of the aircraft came to this salvage dump; Strandtman recovered and returned to flying in early May.

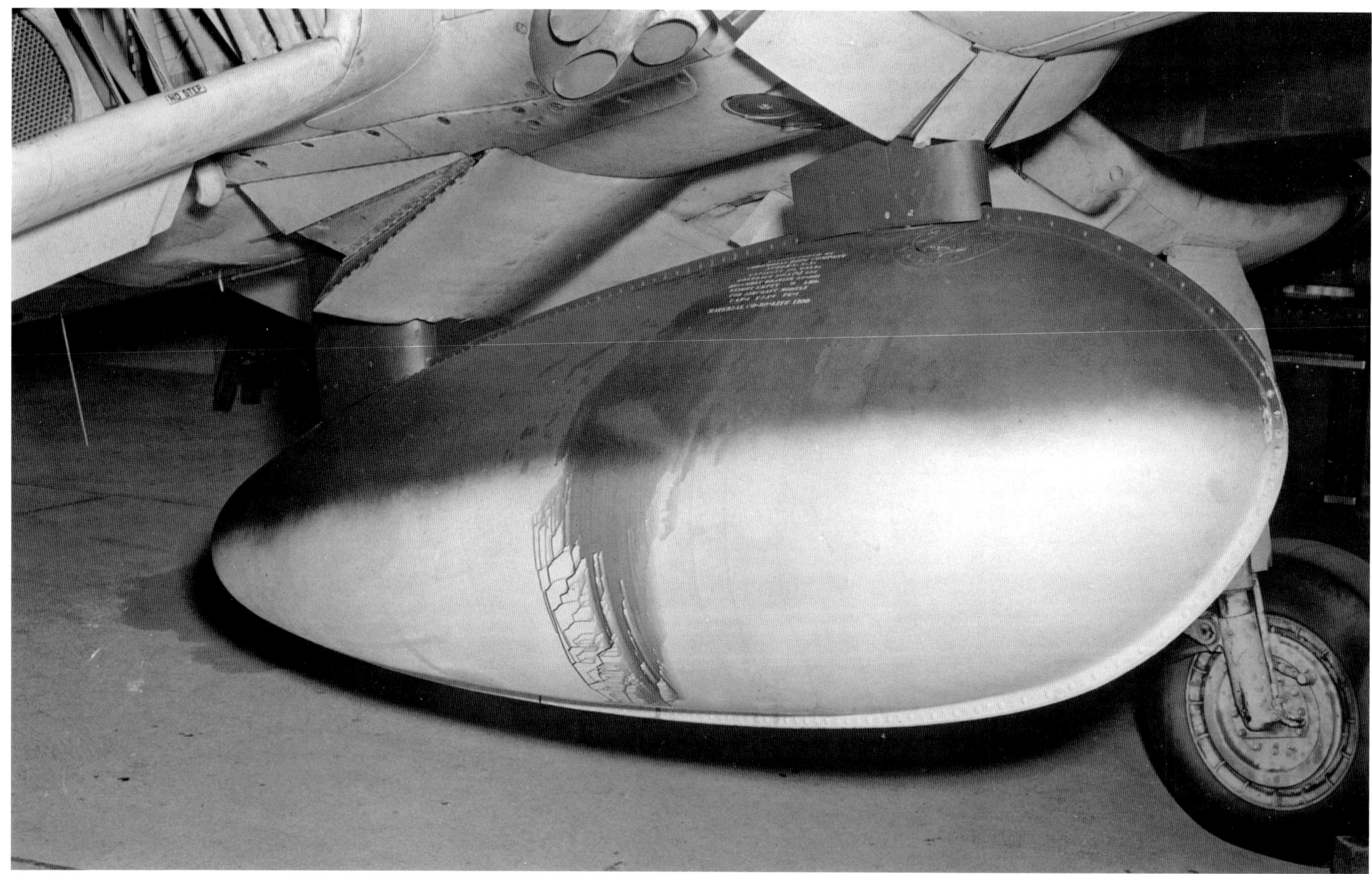

Although in development for most of 1943, Corsairs capable of carrying the centerline fuel tank would not reach the Pacific until early 1944. Duramold produced seamless tanks of resin-impregnated plywood. Columbian Rope Company produced Co-ro-lite tanks using high-impact plastic reinforced with rope fibers. (The Columbian Rope tanks, as seen here, were formed with a vertical flange along the seam.) Goodyear and Brewster produced several metal tank designs with vertical or horizontal flanges at the seams. This tank was photographed during evaluation at Pax River in September 1943.

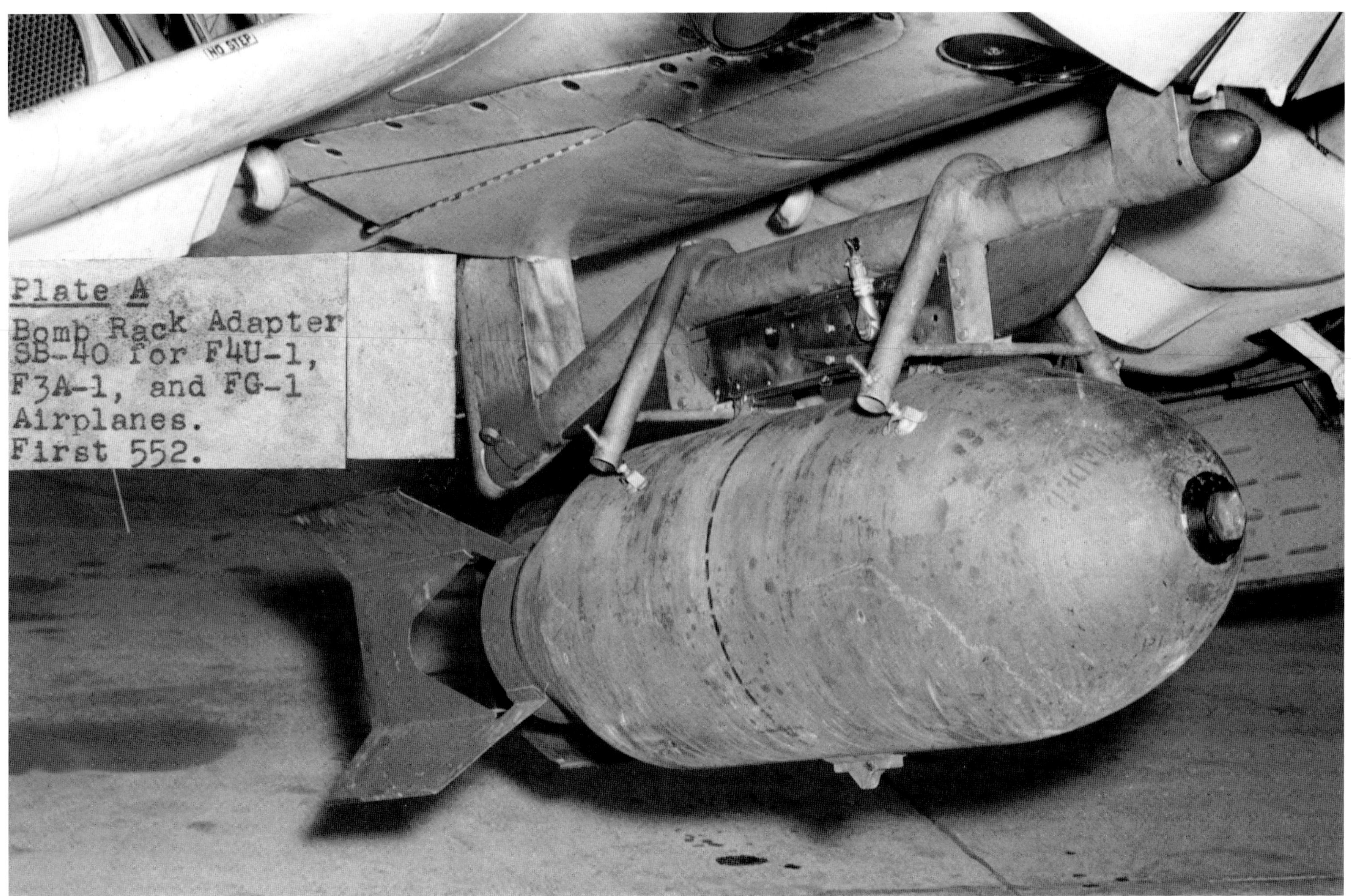

Although crews believed that the Corsair's first centerline bomb racks were invented in the field, the racks were invented and produced by Brewster. This image shows one of the first 552 Brewster modifications of the standard Mark 51 rack, with a 1,000-pound M65 general purpose bomb attached. The odd bend at the rear of the frame allowed the ventral intercooler air exit flap to operate without interference. September 1944.

The Marine Corps first requested its own aircraft carriers in 1926, but the first dedicated Marine Air Support Group would not form until late 1944. Comprising the escort carriers *USS Block Island CVE-106*, *Gilbert Islands CVE-107*, *Vella Gulf CVE-111*, and (seen here) *Cape Gloucester CVE-109*, Carrier Division 27 saw its first combat in July 1945. Although created to support Marine ground forces, an unrelated fighter sweep in the South China Sea allowed four VMF-351 pilots to score five victories over Japanese aircraft; one of those victories is represented below the cockpit of FG-1D FF51 in September 1945.

The five-inch HVAR proved to be an effective ground-attack weapon. Here, marine armament crews load the rockets onto a VMF-511 F4U-1D on board Block Island prior to a June 1945 mission against O Shima.

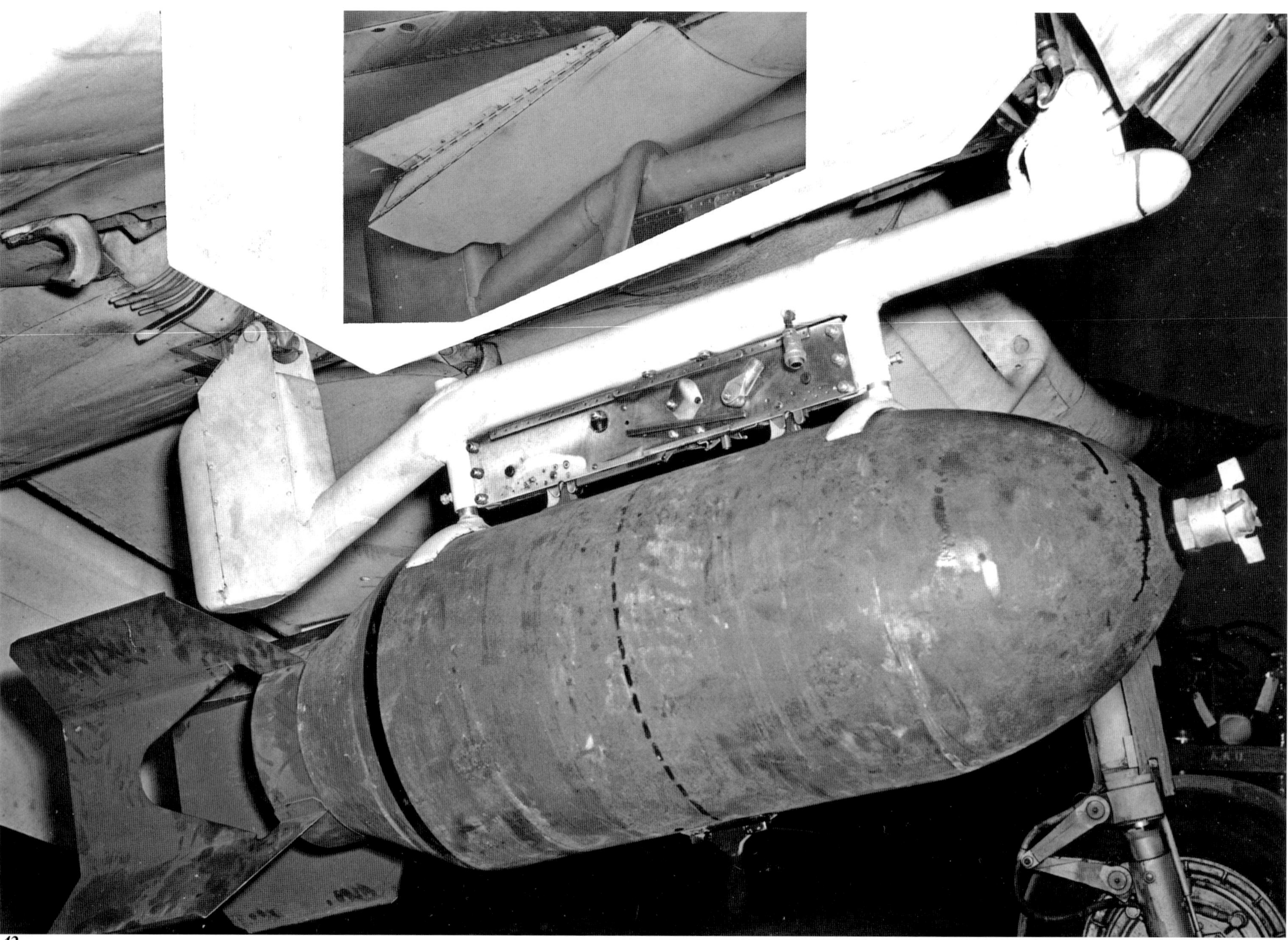

(Previous Page) Brewster switched to this simpler design with its 553rd rack. BuAer planned to have Goodyear also produce 1000 bomb rack adapters, but those plans were dropped due to the company's other commitments. The Brewster racks were carried by Corsairs built by all three companies. Both of these images show taped in captions and whitened areas from the original Navy report; at the top of this image, a detail view shows a cutout added to the intercooler flap trailing edge. February 1944.

(Above) When F4U-1D prototype BuNo 18108 crashed during the test program at Pax River, the Navy's first production example (BuNo 50360) took it place. (Ten earlier "-1Ds" had already been built for the Fleet Air Arm as Corsair IIs JT555 through JT564.) Photographed on 1 August 1944, 50360 carries a Lockheed P-38 165-gallon tank on the right-hand pylon and a 1,000-pound general purpose bomb on the left. Note the graded camouflage scheme – the overall Glossy Sea Blue scheme would not be introduced for another 300 aircraft.

Vought technicians prepare an R-2800-8 Double Wasp engine for installation in an F4U-1 in 1943. Note the horseshoe crab shape of the early unpressurized distributor (below the technician's right hand) and the attached tubular steel ignition harness - a combination seen on all Corsairs into early 1944.

The *USS Essex CV-9* hoists aboard a replacement F4U-1D on 4 February 1945. At the time, the carrier flew two Marine Corsair squadrons, VMF-124 and VMF-213. This aircraft carries a 165-gallon Lockheed fuel tank on each pylon, with a 160-gallon tank on the centerline. After leaving Ulithi Lagoon, the *Essex* air group would strike Tokyo on 16-17 February – the first attacks on the Japanese capital since the Doolittle Raid almost three years earlier.

LEFT
WING
RIGHT
EMERGENCY
RELEASE
BOMB & DROP TANK
ARM
NOSE & TAIL
TAIL
SAFE
TO
TAIL
PULL
CAUTION
CO_2 EMERGENCY
LANDING GEAR RELEASE
CARBON DIOXIDE CYL.

(Top left) Although several different bomb shackles were tested, most production aircraft used the AN-B-10 rack seen here.

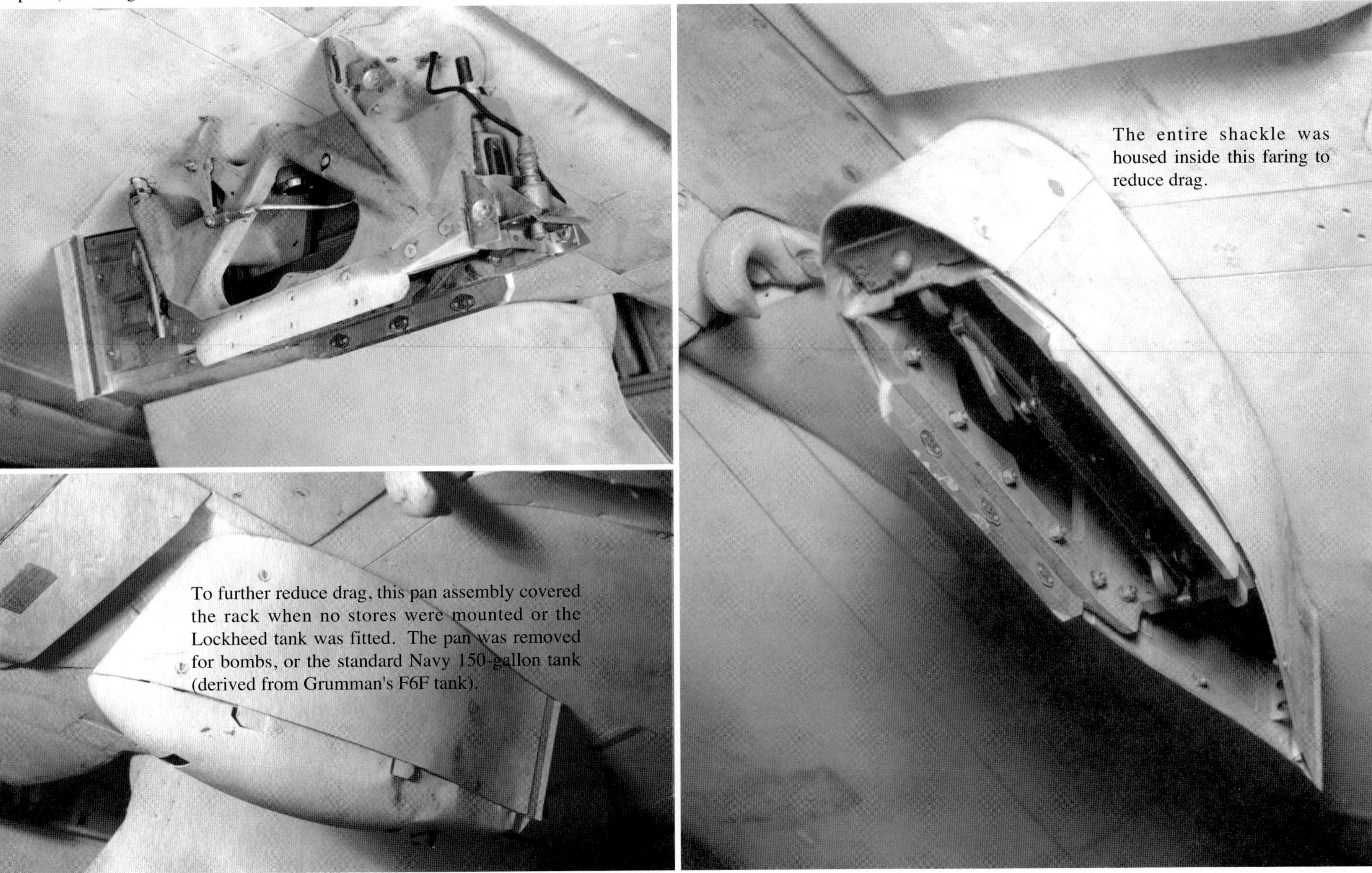

The entire shackle was housed inside this faring to reduce drag.

To further reduce drag, this pan assembly covered the rack when no stores were mounted or the Lockheed tank was fitted. The pan was removed for bombs, or the standard Navy 150-gallon tank (derived from Grumman's F6F tank).

(Previous Page - Top) With the addition of the pylon bomb racks, arming and release switches were added to the right side of the cockpit coaming. (Switches on the left side controlled the guns and gun sight.) The first three switches (as also seen inside the rear cover) armed and prepare each pylon bomb for release; the actual drop was triggered by a red button atop the control stick. This aircraft has a fourth switch to the right, installed to enable an electrical drop of a centerline bomb. (Previous Page - Bottom) When bombs or fuel tanks could not be dropped electrically, a release to the pilot's left could drop the stores manually. The original release pulled used two pins from the holes at the top of the housing; this aircraft has a newer release lever mounted on the side.

Desperate for reconnaissance aircraft, the Navy and Marines experimented with a variety of Corsair camera installations. Little is known of the story of this aircraft (BuNo 17929) other than it was photographed taking off from Empress Augusta Bay in January 1944, and it appears to have oblique camera ports behind the wing and in the fuselage star.

(Upper right) Another mystery, this South Pacific image has a camera being installed in the after service hatch. (Lower left) Two images of a similar mount created by VMF-111 in June 1944. A single K-21 camera and 7-inch lens were mounted in the aft fuselage, with a port cut through the hatch. (Lower right) MAG-22 built a K-25 camera mount into the hatch, using it on all the group's photographic aircraft during strikes on Ponape in October 1944.

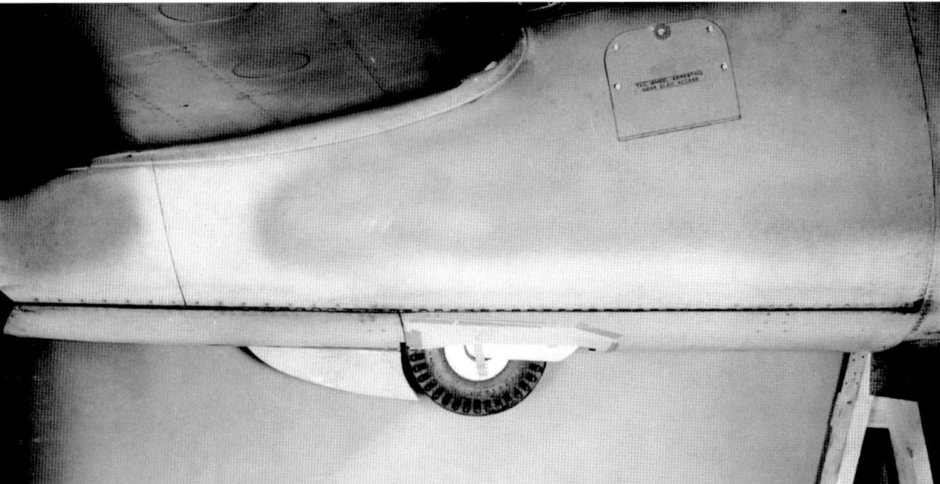

(Top left) Fitted with the Goodyear welded tail wheel extension (see Aircraft Pictorial 7, page 42), this F4U-1A has its tail gear doors cut away for partial retraction. (Top right) Another F4U-1A, this time with the original pneumatic tail wheel and a different cutout through the doors. The fairing fitted behind the tire helped reduce drag. Note the panel line through the tail gear doors; each door was divided into a forward and an after section that were normally linked. (Lower) This VMF-451 FG-1A crashed at Trona Field, California, on 3 August 1944 when its landing gear collapsed. BuNo 14127 was delivered with several weight- and drag-saving features, including non-folding wings, deleted arrester hook, and faired-over tail cone. Note that only the forward portions of the tail gear doors were opened.

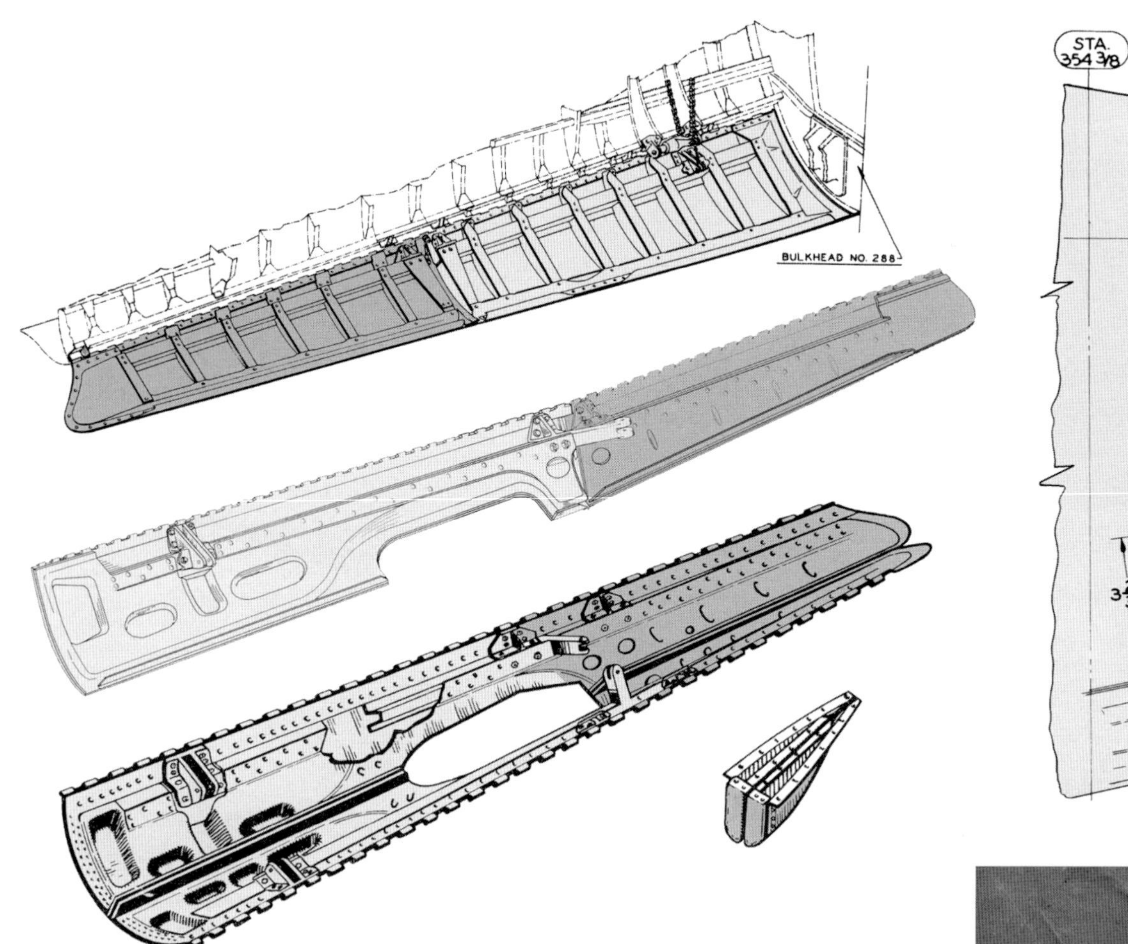

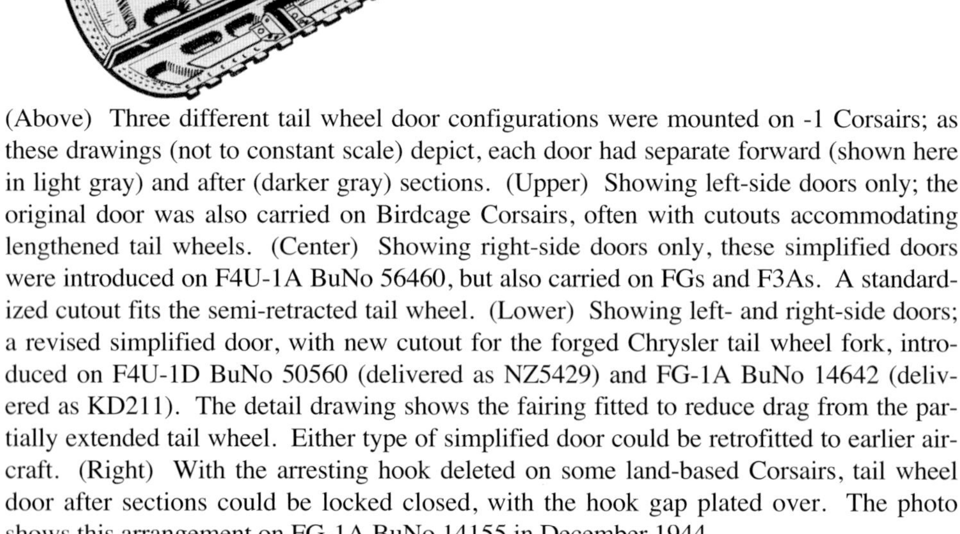

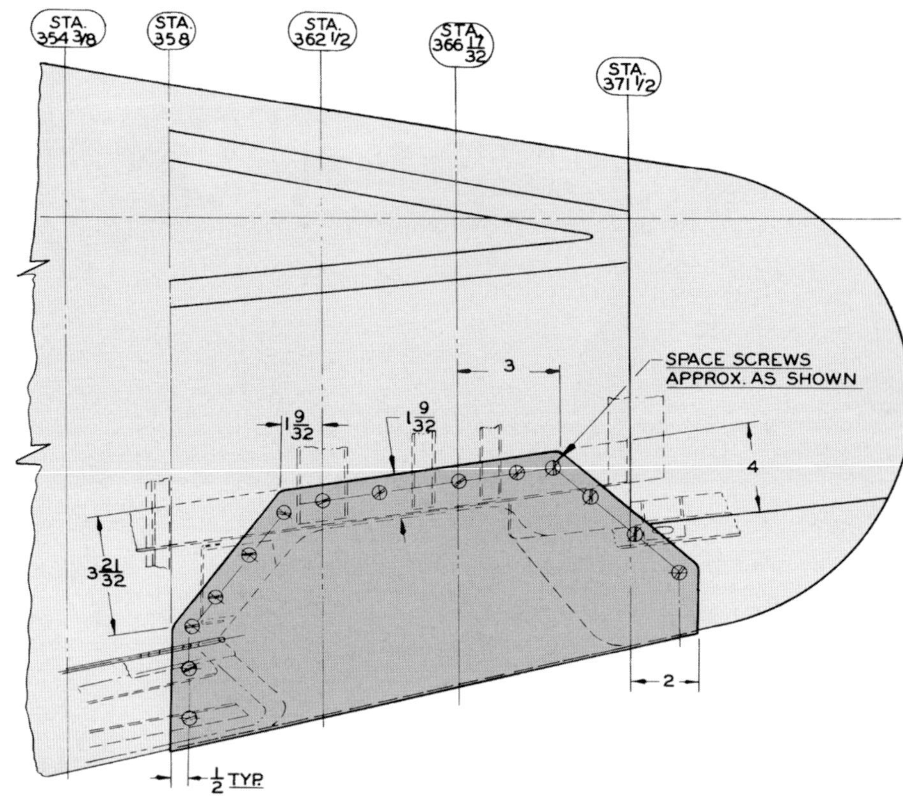

(Above) Three different tail wheel door configurations were mounted on -1 Corsairs; as these drawings (not to constant scale) depict, each door had separate forward (shown here in light gray) and after (darker gray) sections. (Upper) Showing left-side doors only; the original door was also carried on Birdcage Corsairs, often with cutouts accommodating lengthened tail wheels. (Center) Showing right-side doors only, these simplified doors were introduced on F4U-1A BuNo 56460, but also carried on FGs and F3As. A standardized cutout fits the semi-retracted tail wheel. (Lower) Showing left- and right-side doors; a revised simplified door, with new cutout for the forged Chrysler tail wheel fork, introduced on F4U-1D BuNo 50560 (delivered as NZ5429) and FG-1A BuNo 14642 (delivered as KD211). The detail drawing shows the fairing fitted to reduce drag from the partially extended tail wheel. Either type of simplified door could be retrofitted to earlier aircraft. (Right) With the arresting hook deleted on some land-based Corsairs, tail wheel door after sections could be locked closed, with the hook gap plated over. The photo shows this arrangement on FG-1A BuNo 14155 in December 1944.

A prototype fitting of 20mm cannons was made on Birdcage F4U-1 BuNo 02154, photographed here at Pax River in October 1943. As with the .50-caliber wings, the outboard flap was dropped and locked down to improve gun access; depressing a pop-up pin (seen just forward of the outboard edge of the flap) released the lock so that the flap could be manually lifted back into place. The flaps here are the same as used on the .50-caliber wing, though reinforced flaps would soon be introduced to lessen damage from the heavier shell casings.

(Above) The 20mm outer wing panels were similar to the .50-caliber wings, with structural adjustments for the heavier guns and ammo cases. While the thirty sets of spare 20mm wings could easily be mounted on other Corsairs (as recommended by BuAer in January 1945), 47 F4U-1Cs were instead modified back to F4U-1D configuration.

(Right) The 20mm gun barrels were not fitted with blast tubes, instead protruding twenty inches from the leading edge on the outboard gun and thirty inches on the inboard gun.

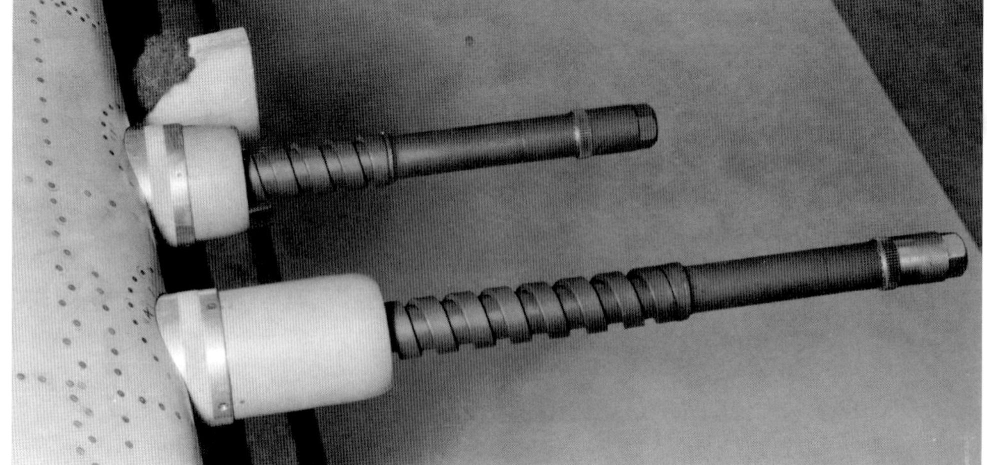

Details... (Upper left) In March 1944, these Marshalls-based MAW-4 marines received a Teddy Bear mascot from actress Barbara Stanwyck. To the left of the group, this Corsair's wing shows a rarely noticed stall warning sensor. (Upper right) The stall sensor was factory installed on F4Us 17930 thru 57643, FGs 13392 thru 76140, and all F3As starting with 04775. A November 1944 bulletin found the stall warning no longer necessary and allowed the system to be removed in the field. (Lower left) An external power receptacle was mounted under the right wing center section, just forward of the flap. (Lower right) A Pacific area modification, used on only a handful of aircraft, moved the receptacle to the right side of the fuselage, just forward of the kick step.

(Left) In common with all -1 Corsairs, FG-1D BuNo 92192 had a flat wing root step on each wing, a D-shaped fuselage kick-step on the right side, and a covered hand grip just below the right side of the windscreen. To improve access, BuAer requested a number of changes in 1944. A kick step was added to the inboard right flap beginning on F4U BuNo 82527 and FG BuNo 87872; the step was originally fitted with a flush cover, which was ordered removed after the war. A diagonal hand grip was added to the fuselage right side (seen a couple of feet forward of the number "69") beginning with F4U BuNo 57981 and FG BuNo 76340. And a hand grip was added at the left side of the windscreen beginning on F4U BuNo 57483 and FG BuNo 76140 (and retrofitted to many earlier aircraft. The rectangular intake below the national insignia added to both sides of the fuselage beginning on FG-1D BuNo 92341 (with retrofit orders for earlier aircraft) to force carbon monoxide from the aft fuselage. (Right) An adjustable jury strut supported wings folded completely or (as seen here) vertically. The strut was attached to a wing fitting forward of the inboard ammo boxes and a fuselage fitting at the firewall.

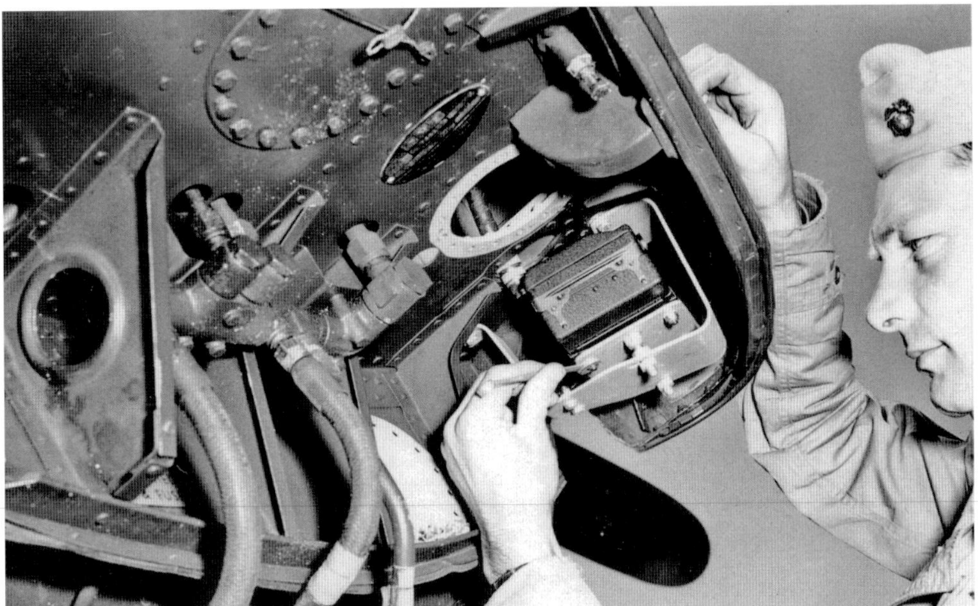

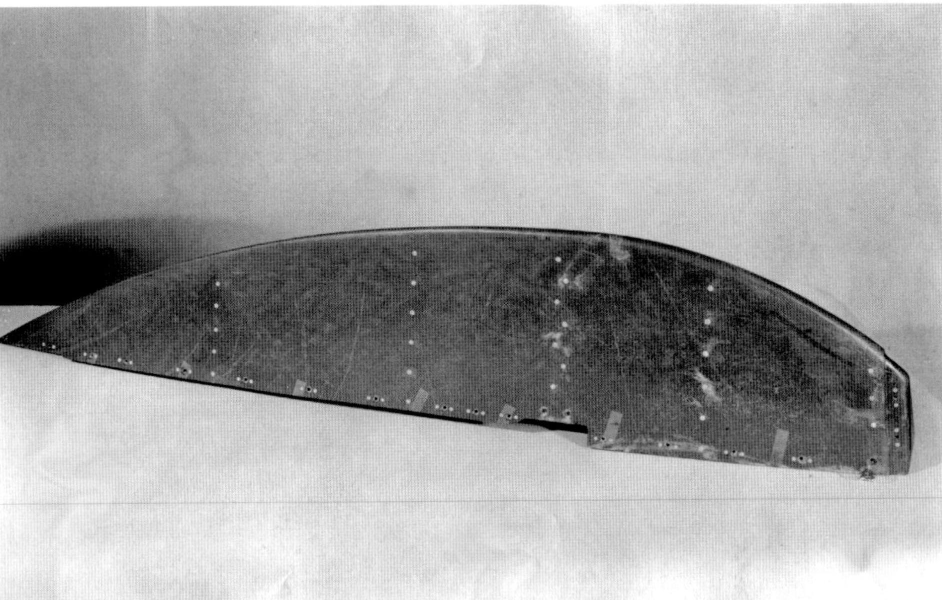

(Upper left) A gun camera was mounted at the root of the right outer wing panel. Easily accessed when the wings were folded, it could also be reached through a small ventral hatch when the wings were lowered.

(Upper right) In mid-1944, BuAer began developing plastic wingtips for US aircraft. Easily replaced when damaged, the removable tips entered production on F4U BuNo 57567 and FG BuNo 76446.

(Lower) In February 1945, the Pacific fleet began color-coding the ammo boxes for its carrier-based Corsairs. On the left wing, the sides of the boxes were painted red, with a 2-inch black stripe distinguishing the shorter number 2 box. Side of the right wing boxes were left Interior Green (or zinc chromate yellow) as delivered from the factory, with a black stripe distinguishing the shorter number 4 box.

This March 1944 images shows a Mark 5 rocket installation tested under the wing of F4U-1A BuNo 55919. The Mark 5 launcher, which accommodated 3.5-inch or 5-inch rockets, would be standardized for Corsairs that summer. Though the rockets were originally launched sequentially from the outboard positions, the order was reversed in March 1945 to clear the positions over the machine gun ejector chutes. (With links and shells damaging the rockets below, guns could not be used until the two inboard rockets had been fired.) The special paint job includes one launcher stub in Insignia Blue and two stubs divided in White and Insignia Blue.

To protect the wing from rocket blast, the outboard flap and part of the outer panel underside were reskinned with sheet aluminum. This image shows 3.5 inch rockets refitted with 5-inch warheads.

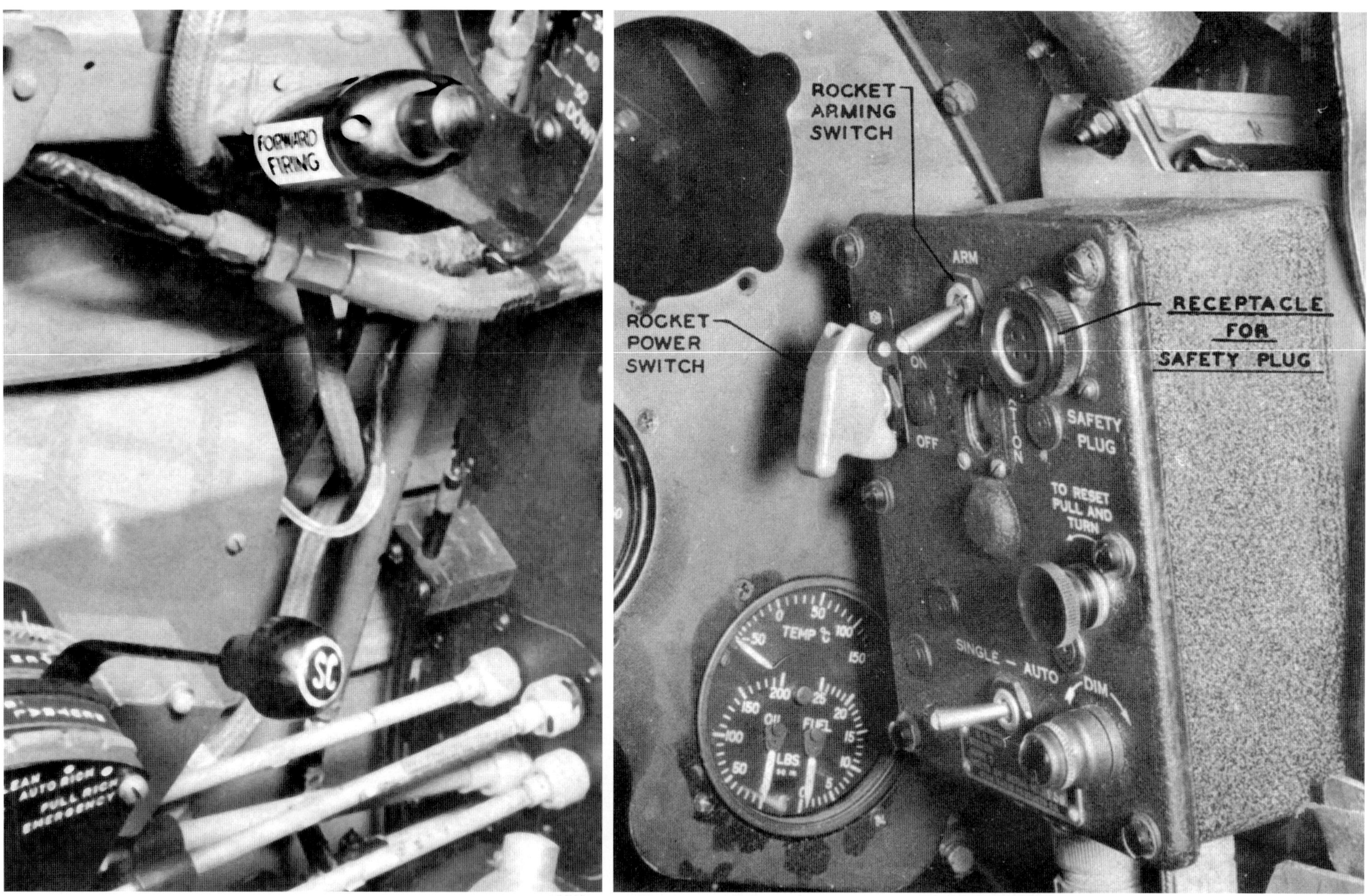

Corsair rocket launch controls included (right) a Mark 3 station distributor box to the right of the instrument panel and (left) a dedicated firing switch behind the flap position indicator. The entire system was activated by the master armament switch atop the instrument panel coaming. In February 1945, BuAer planned to move the firing button to the joy stick on FG-1Ds, but post-war photos suggest this was rarely done.

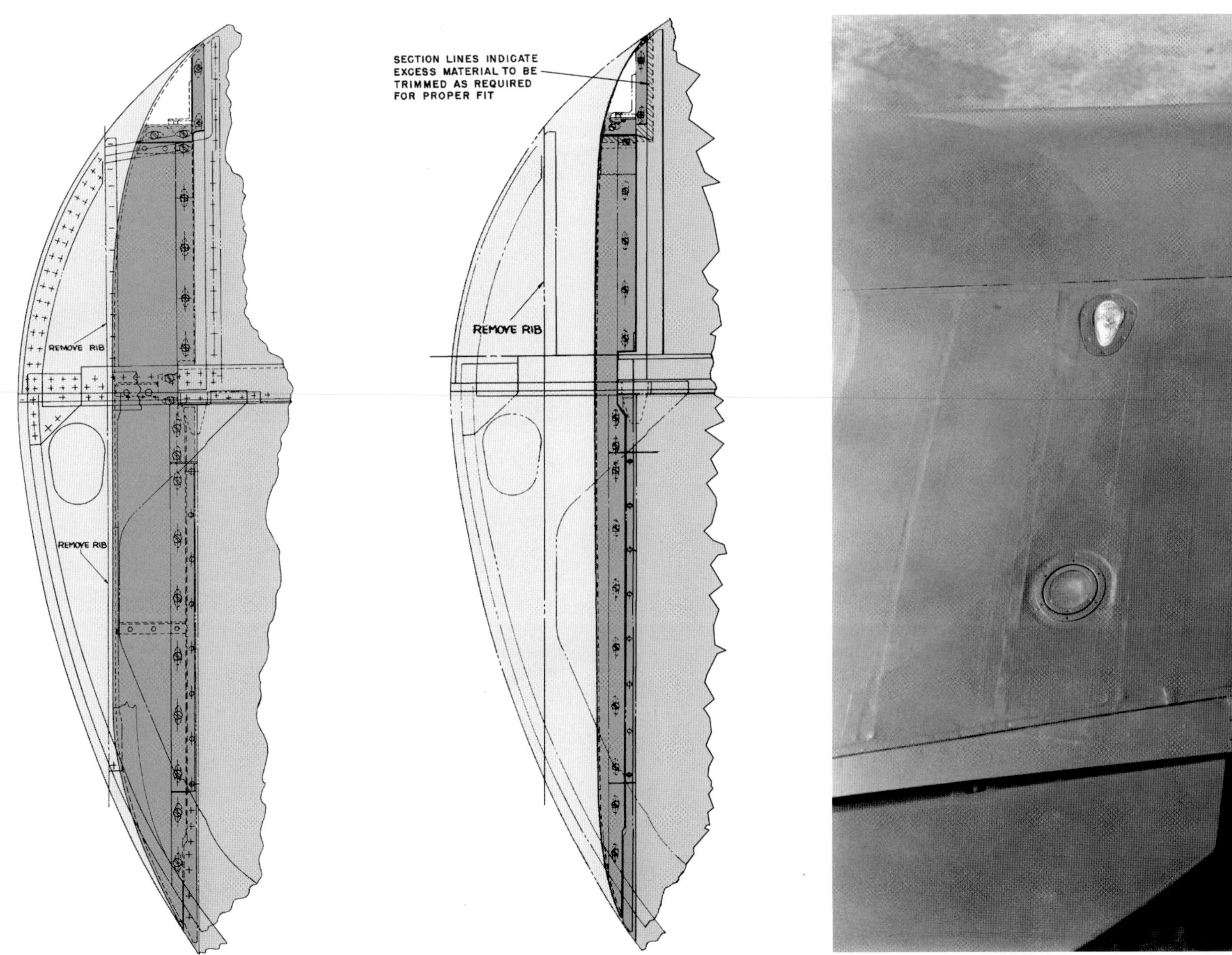

The drawing above, left, shows the short Andover Kent fiberglass wingtips installed on Corsair marks I, II, and III. The right-hand drawing shows the "short short" wingtip retrofitted to Corsairs II and III and factory installed on all Corsair Mark IVs. The pale gray areas represent the outline of the original US Navy Corsair wing, with the darkest gray showing the replacement tips. The photo shows a short short wingtip as installed on Corsair IV KD365 in September 1944.

In early 1944, British trials at Boscombe Down revealed unacceptable carbon monoxide levels in the Corsair cockpit. An aerodynamic fluke allowed the poisonous gas accumulating in the aft fuselage to be forced into the cockpit by pressure differentials. While the US Navy initially countered the problem by improving the seals around bulkhead 218, the British requested intake vents on either side of the fuselage, with an ventral exhaust extractor. All three manufacturers would eventually add the fittings in production, with kits produced for field installation on earlier aircraft. The photos above show the right side intake (left) and the exhaust extractor (right) on an early Goodyear Corsair IV.

In just under three months, VF-17's Lieutenant Ira C. Kepford scored sixteen aerial victories. In his final combat on 19 February 1944, Kepford scored three victories, but his own aircraft was heavily damaged and never flew again. This F4U-1A (BuNo 562##) was one of at least two Corsairs painted up to publicized the ace's successes before he returned to the US in March. The stub of the broken MHF antenna mast is visible on the forward fuselage; the aerial has been rewired from behind the canopy to the right stabilizer tip and up to the rudder top. Similarly, the broken VHF antenna mast has been replaced with a simple whip antenna. The fuselage camouflage on this aircraft uses a gradual stippling of Sea Blue into White with no transition through Intermediate Blue.

(Upper) VMF-114 flew its "land plane" FG-1As (note the enclosed arresting hook positions) to Peleliu on 17 September 1944, providing close air support for the marine forces there until the island was secured. This 17 October photo shows BuNo 14214 taxiing past BuNo 14104 at the beginning of another short mission – Japanese positions were only a few hundred yards from the fighter strip. Note the squadron's white cowl ring, propeller shaft, and tail tip markings.

(Lower) Parked on an inclined hardstand at Barakoma Field – with rocks to keep her from rolling back into the taxiway – Mary-Jo was an F4U-1A (BuNo 17911) assigned to VMF-212. At the time – January 1944 – the squadron was flying operations against the Japanese stronghold at Rabaul.

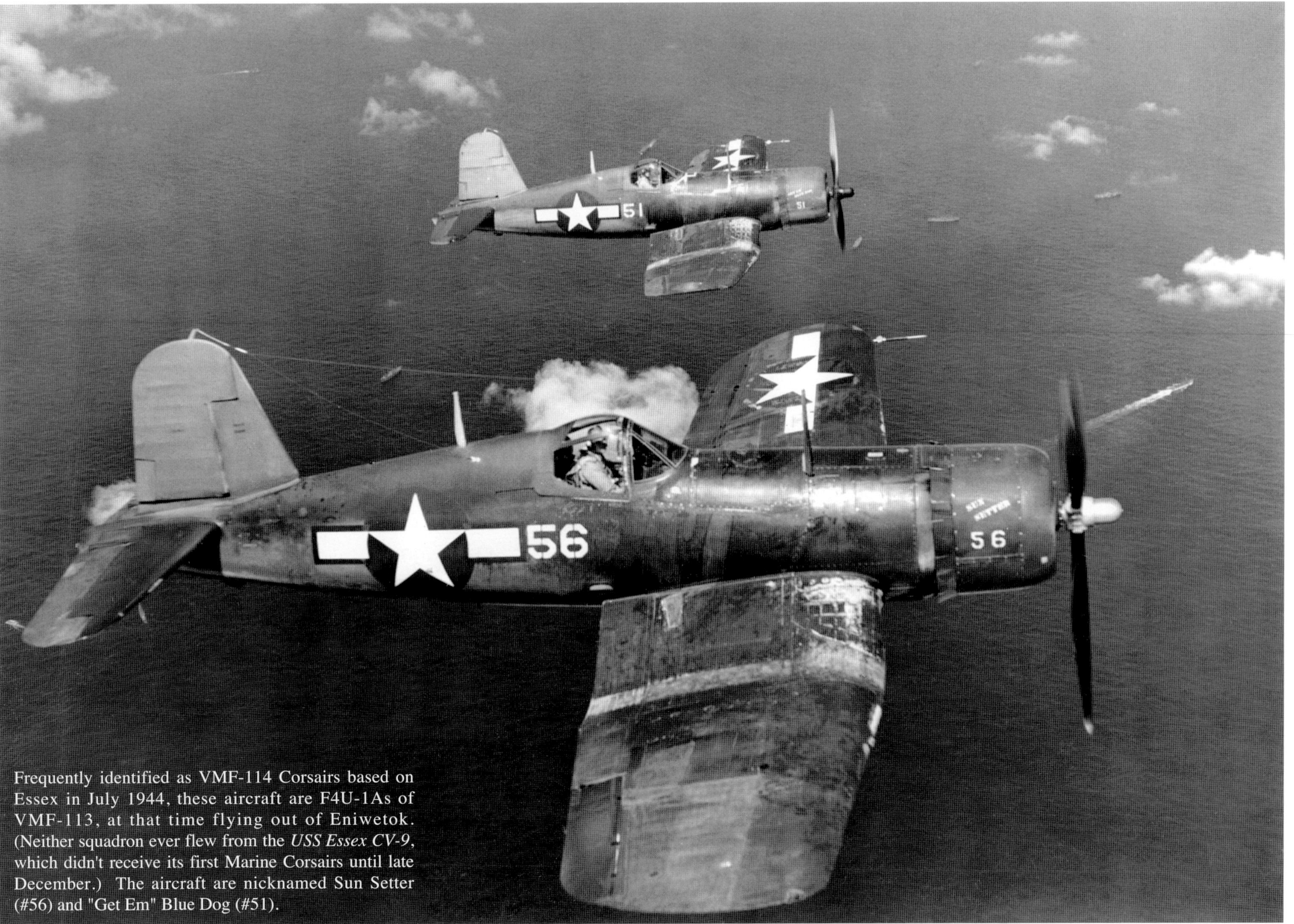

Frequently identified as VMF-114 Corsairs based on Essex in July 1944, these aircraft are F4U-1As of VMF-113, at that time flying out of Eniwetok. (Neither squadron ever flew from the *USS Essex CV-9*, which didn't receive its first Marine Corsairs until late December.) The aircraft are nicknamed Sun Setter (#56) and "Get Em" Blue Dog (#51).

In January 1945, Bunker Hill became the first carrier to embark three squadrons of Corsairs. VF-84, VMF-221, and VMF-451 all flew yellow-nosed F4U-1Ds for the first fast carrier air strikes against Tokyo a month later. By the time of this April 1945 photo, the yellow noses had been repainted as the carrier participated in the Okinawa invasion. One month later, Bunker Hill would be hit by kamikazes and put out of action for the remainder of the war. This image features a rarely seen reconnaissance-configured Corsair – note the partially opened camera port in the center of number 171's fuselage star.

Its contract cancelled in May 1944, Brewster would deliver only 735 Corsairs. Most (430) went to Britain, with the remaining 305 used in training roles by US forces. This F3A-1A was photographed in January 1946.

Another F3A-1A, BuNo 11196 was assigned to VMF-123 during a cross-country flight on 29 October 1944. When the prop ran away on take-off from Laramie, Wyoming, the pilot brought the aircraft down three-quarters of a mile from the runway's end; the main gear sheared off before it was fully extended, and though the aircraft skidded for 460 feet, there was remarkably little damage.

(Right) A somewhat casual application of white stripes marked the nose and tail of this VMF-121 FG-1A (BuNo 13754), which crashed at Mojave in May 1944. (Below) Another landing gear problem at MCAS Mojave, this time in August 1944. The checkerboard application to this VMF-124 FG-1A (L63, BuNo 13644) was a good bit neater. Both aircraft wore graded camouflage, though L63 has a distinct pattern of Intermediate Blue on the fuselage.

In 1946, the Naval Air Reserve Training Command created a new marking system for its aircraft. Glossy Sea Blue fighters, such as the Corsair, were to receive a 22-inch fuselage band and 24x30-inch fuselage and underwing numbers, with all markings (except the national insignia) in the same Orange Yellow the Navy had used to paint prewar wings. (Upper) FG-1D BuNo 88369 crashed just outside of NAS Grosse Ile on 3 October 1946. (Lower) Although the Reserve markings were officially changed in late 1946, FG-1D BuNo 92094 was still wearing the older system when it crashed on 16 March 1947.

BuAer spent much of 1946 trying to convince Naval Air Reserve Training Command to adopt a marking system of BuAer's design; by year's end the argument was over. Photographed on 6 March 1949, FG-1D BuNo 92678 displays the revised markings: the national insignia was reapplied on the fuselage, with an International Orange band sized to fit the star. Each field was identified by a code letter – in this case "I" for Grosse Ile.

TABULATED DATA

WING	
DIDHEDRAL OUTER PANEL	8 1/2°
SWEEPBACK AT 30% CHORD	0°
INCIDENCE	2°
MEAN AERODYNAMIC CHORD	94"
DISTANCE FROM L.E. CENTER SECTION	3.6"
DISTANCE BELOW THRUST LINE	20.1"
NORMAL INCIDENCE OF STABILIZER	+1 1/4°
WHEEL & TIRE SIZE	32 x 8
TAIL WHEEL SIZE (PNEUMATIC)	12 1/2 x 4 1/2
WING AREA INCLUDING AILERONS & 37.7 SQ. FT. OF FUSELAGE AREA	314 SQ. FT.
AILERON AREA TOTAL (AFT OF HINGE LINE) NORMAL TO REF. PLANE	18.1 SQ. FT.
FLAP AREA TOTAL (AFT OF HINGE LINE) NORMAL TO REF. PLANE	36.36 SQ. FT.
OUTER PANEL	15.13 SQ. FT.
CENTER SECTION (PLAN VIEW)	21.23 SQ. FT.

TOTAL HORIZONTAL TAIL SURFACE AREA	57.9 SQ. FT.
STABILIZER AREA INCLUDING 3.5 SQ. FT. OF FUSELAGE AREA FORWARD OF ELEVATOR HINGE ℄, 2.7 SQ. FT. OF CONTAINED ELEVATOR BALANCE AREA, & 1.2 SQ. FT. OF FUSELAGE AREA AFT OF ELEVATOR HINGE ℄	36 SQ. FT.
ELEVATOR AREA INCLUDING 0.74 SQ. FT. OF BALANCE TAB AND 1.36 SQ. FT. OF TRIM TAB AREA	21.9 SQ. FT.
TOTAL VERTICAL TAIL SURFACE AREA	22.0 SQ. FT.
FIN AREA INCLUDING 0.86 SQ. FT. OF FIN AREA AFT OF RUDDER HINGE ℄, AND 1.66 SQ. FT. OF CONTAINED RUDDER BALANCE AREA	9 SQ. FT.
RUDDER AREA, INCLUDING 0.85 SQ. FT. OF TAB AREA	13 SQ. FT.
ANGULAR MOVEMENTS	
FLAPS (ALSO USED FOR MANEUVERING)	50° (ENG. REF. ONLY)
AILERON	UP 19° DOWN 14°
TAB-LEFT AILERON	UP 15° DOWN 15°
ELEVATORS (SEE NOTE #1)	UP 24° DOWN 16°
TAB	UP 10° DOWN 20°
RUDDER (SEE NOTE #1)	±25°
TAB	±18°

THE RELATIONSHIP BETWEEN THE PRESELECTED FLAP HANDLE SETTING & THE RESULTING FLAP ANGLE SHALL BE WITHIN ±7° EXCEPT THAT FULL UP & DOWN MUST BE OBTAINED.

AIRFOIL DESIGNATION
- CENTER SECTION NACA 23018 AT ROOT TO 23015
- OUTER PANEL NACA 23015 AT ROOT TO 23009 AT TIP
- HORIZONTAL TAIL SURFACE - CV SPECIAL
- VERTICAL TAIL SURFACE - CV SPECIAL

NOTE: TOLERANCE ON ELEVATOR & RUDDER ANGULAR MOVEMENTS ±1°
ALL TRIM TAB MOTION TOLERANCES ARE ±1°
THE AILERON MOTION TOLERANCES WILL BE AS FOLLOWS: UP ±1° DOWN ±1°

PLACE CONTOUR BOARDS NEAR THE MID-SPAN OF THE AILERON AND FLAP TO CHECK ALIGNMENT OF TRAILING EDGE.
DEVIATION OF THE TRAILING EDGE FROM THE CONTOUR BOARD SHALL NOT EXCEED ± 1/4" FOR THE FLAPS OR ± 5/32" FOR THE AILERONS.

LINK BALANCED TAB MOTIONS
TAB UP (AILERON DOWN 14°) 26° ±1° } REFER TO MEDIAM
TAB DOWN (AILERON UP 19°) 38° ± 1° } LINE OF AILERON
ADJUST END ON PUSH ROD VS-24016 (REF) TO PROVIDE ± 4° TRIM ADJUSTMENT FOR TAB (AILERON NEUTRAL)

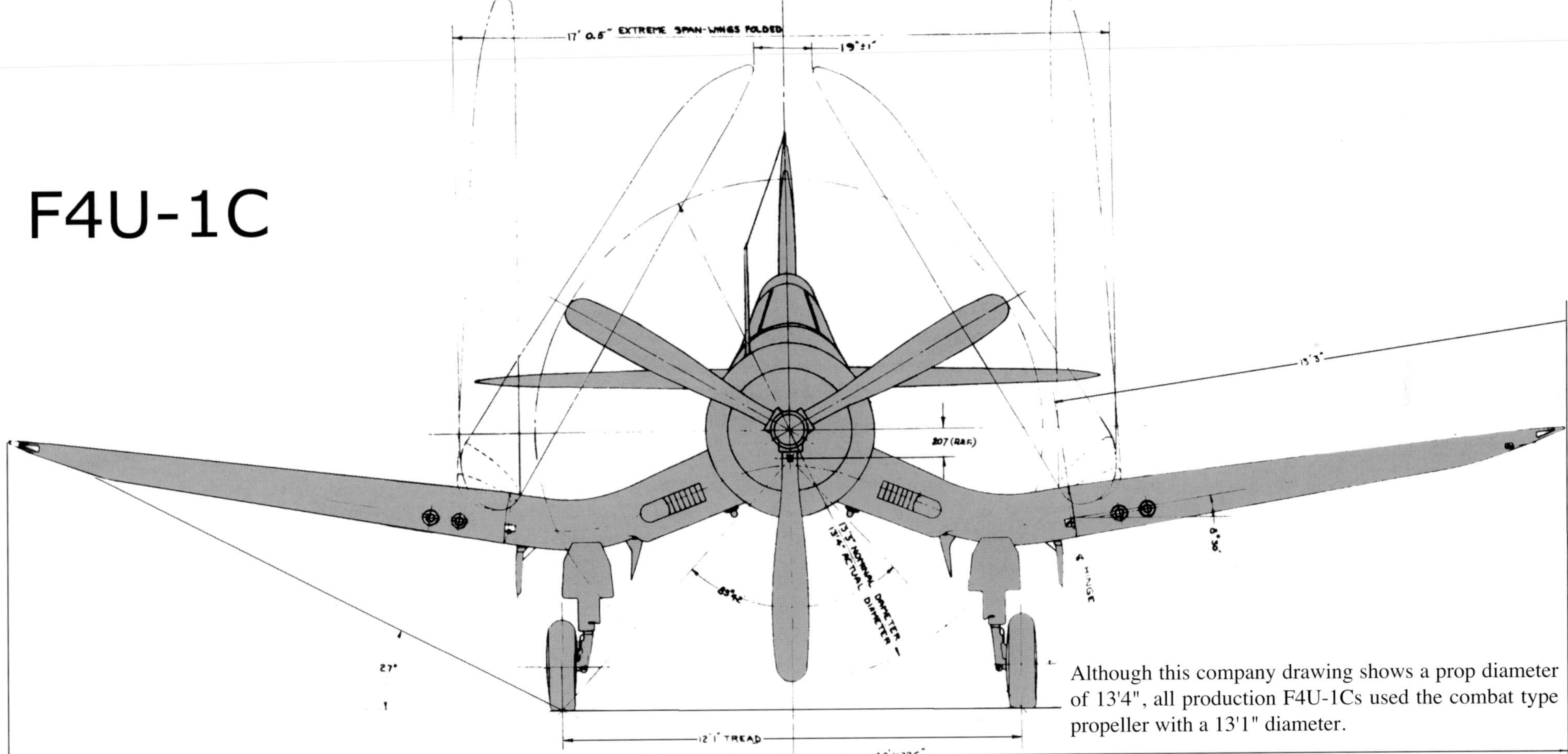

Although this company drawing shows a prop diameter of 13'4", all production F4U-1Cs used the combat type propeller with a 13'1" diameter.

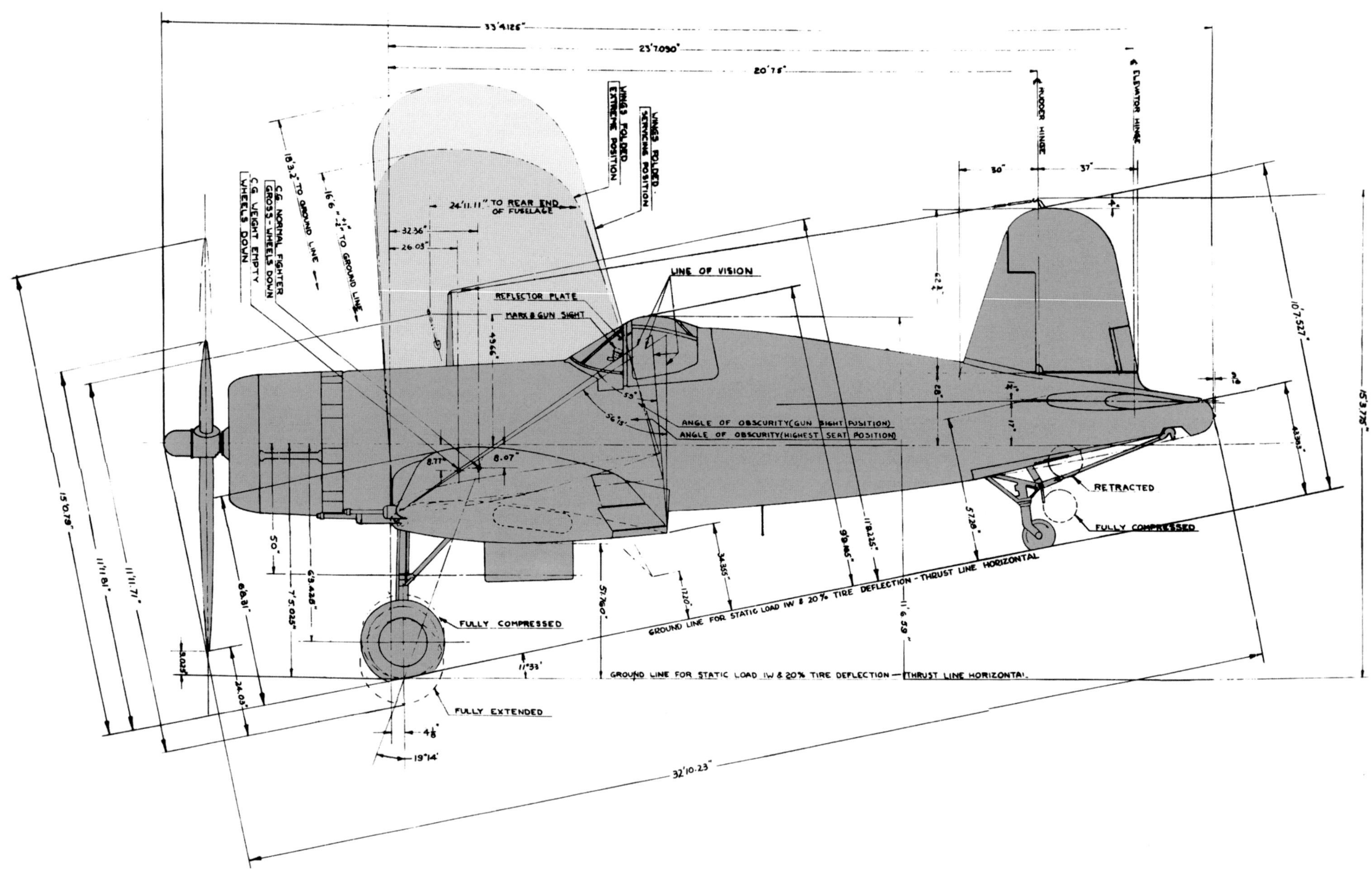

33'4.125"
23'7.090"
20'7.5"
WINGS FOLDED EXTREME POSITION
WINGS FOLDED SERVICING POSITION
RUDDER HINGE
ELEVATOR HINGE
24'11.11" TO REAR END OF FUSELAGE
LINE OF VISION
REFLECTOR PLATE
MARK 8 GUN SIGHT
ANGLE OF OBSCURITY (GUN SIGHT POSITION)
ANGLE OF OBSCURITY (HIGHEST SEAT POSITION)
C.G. NORMAL FIGHTER GROSS-WHEELS DOWN
C.G. WEIGHT EMPTY WHEELS DOWN
RETRACTED
FULLY COMPRESSED
FULLY EXTENDED
GROUND LINE FOR STATIC LOAD IW & 20% TIRE DEFLECTION - THRUST LINE HORIZONTAL
32'10.23"
15'3.75"
10'7.527"
15'0.78"

Tail light. The aft end of the fuselage held a white light that served double duty as a running light and recognition light. The dome covering the light could be replaced on the ground, with clear, red, and green domes available for each aircraft.

Landing light. A sealed-beam landing light was mounted flush beneath the left wing of all early Corsairs. The light rotated forward to illuminate the area ahead during landings and takeoffs, but proved of limited value. By mid-1943, BuAer had decided to delete the light in production, beginning with F4U BuNo 56266 and FG BuNo 76140. The mount for the light was originally covered by an aluminum disc, though the entire structure was eventually redesigned and covered with fabric.

Approach light. The approach light was mounted on the leading edge of all Corsairs, inboard of the left wing guns. Used for carrier landings, the light helped the carrier's landing signal officer determine the aircraft's position on the glide path. After the war, the signal was modified to satisfy the "latest landing technique aboard carriers," though that modification was internal and adjusted only the angle at which the approach light could be viewed.

Recognition lights. Raised cabin aircraft were introduced with four recognition lights on the right wing. Below the wing were three flush, circular lights, tinted red, green, and amber from the leading edge. Above the right wing was a single white teardrop light, which was scheduled for deletion in mid-1944. Vought began deleting the upper light with BuNo 57781 (though many subsequent aircraft were delivered with the light), and Goodyear began deleting on 87988. (The light was present on all Brewster Corsairs.) Postwar Corsairs saw many local deletions on the three underwing lights, often with simple fabric patches covering the holes.

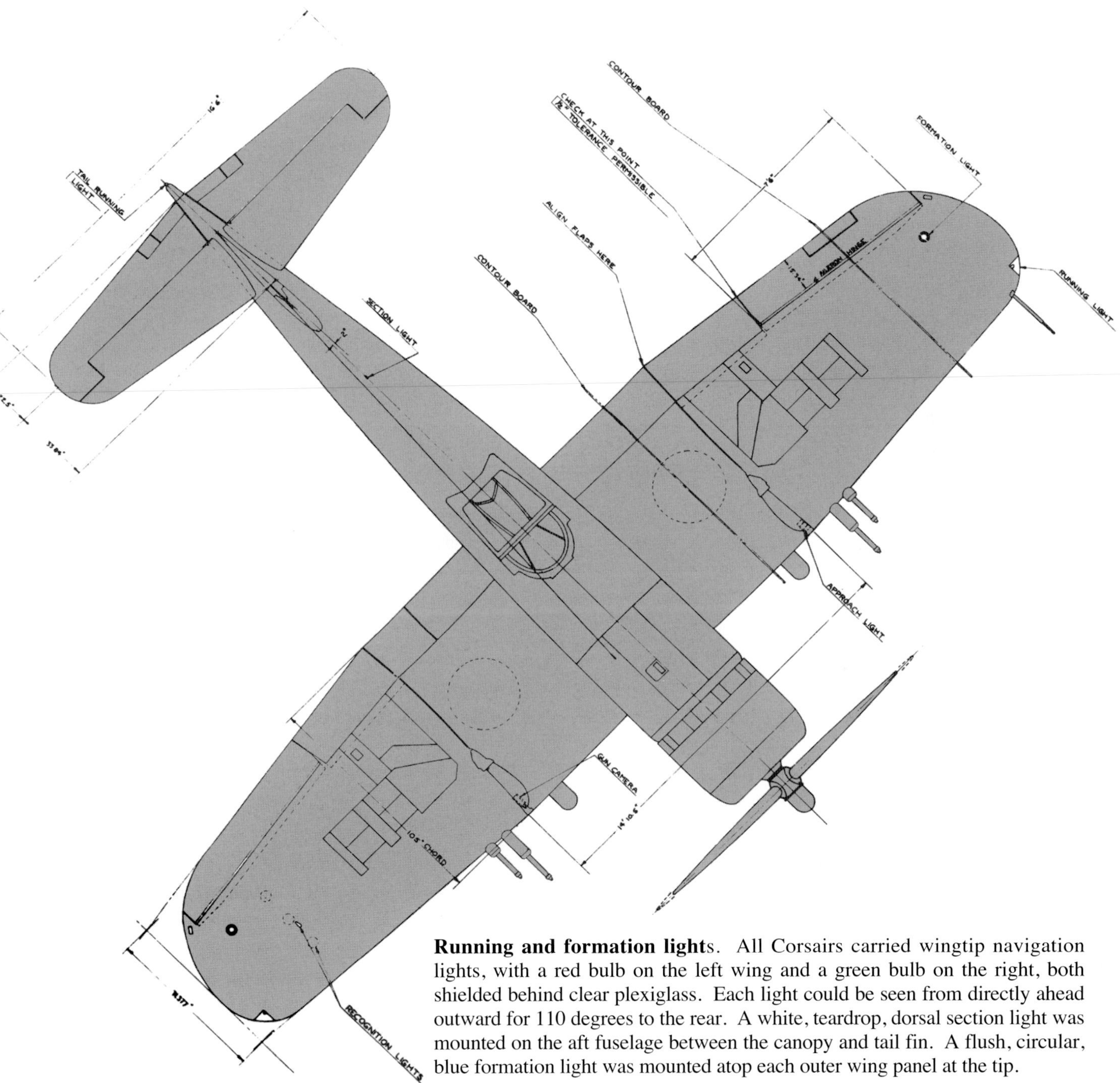

Running and formation lights. All Corsairs carried wingtip navigation lights, with a red bulb on the left wing and a green bulb on the right, both shielded behind clear plexiglass. Each light could be seen from directly ahead outward for 110 degrees to the rear. A white, teardrop, dorsal section light was mounted on the aft fuselage between the canopy and tail fin. A flush, circular, blue formation light was mounted atop each outer wing panel at the tip.

ADDITIONAL READING

US Marine Corps Fighter Squadrons of World War II
B. Tillman, Osprey Publishing, 2014
US Navy Fighter Squadrons in World War II
B. Tillman, Specialty Press, 1997
The Vought F4U Corsair: A Comprehensive Guide
R. Morrissey & J. Hegedus, SAM Publications, 2010
History of Marine Corps Aviation in World War II
R. Sherrod, Nautical & Aviation Publishing, 1987
The Time Capsule Fighter: Corsair KD431
D. Morris, Sutton Publishing, 2006
F4U Corsair in Action
J. Sullivan, Squadron/Signal Publications, 2013
Corsair: The Saga of the Legendary Bent-Wing Fighter-Bomber
W. A. Musciano, Schiffer Publishing, 2009

RESOURCES

NATIONAL AIR & SPACE MUSEUM ARCHIVES
Smithsonian Institution, Washington, DC
E. Borja, D. Schwartz, Allan Janus, Mark Kahn, Brian Nicklas,& K. Igoe
NATIONAL ARCHIVES & RECORDS ADMINISTRATION
Document & Photographic Collections
Archives I, Washington, DC
Archives II, College Park, MD
H. Reed
NATIONAL AERONAUTICS & SPACE ADMINISTRATION
Langley Research Center,
M. Gainer & T. Hornbuckle

Our next AIRCRAFT PICTORIAL:
AAF Colors – Olive Drab & Neutral Gray

ACKNOWLEDGEMENTS

The Author & CWP would like to express their gratitude to the following individuals:
**Bruce Archer • David Doyle • Steven Eisenman
Don Fenton • Alan Griffith • David Hansen
Joe Hegedus • David H. Klaus • Benjamin Kristy
Jim McColey • S. Mesner • Rafe Morrissey
Allan Peters • Stan Piet • Bill Spidle • Jim Sullivan
Roy Sutherland • Wayne Tevlin • Tommy H. Thomason
Barrett Tillman • Larry D. Webster**

AIRCRAFT PICTORIAL SERIES

AP #1 - USS Midway Air Wings
AP #2 - SB2U Vindicator
AP #3 - OS2U Kingfisher
AP #4 - F4F Wildcat
AP #5 - P-40 Warhawk
AP #6 - F-4B/N Phantom II
AP #7 - F4U-1 Corsair Vol. 1
AP #8 - F4U-1 Corsair Vol. 2

Front Cover: Photographed on a test flight over the US, this early F4U-1D carries a pair of 1,000-pound bombs beneath the fuselage.

Title Page: An F4U-1A of VMF-215, reconstituted as an operational training squadron at Ewa, Hawaii, mid-1945.

Back Cover: A VMF-511 armorer preps the guns of his F4U-1D on board the escort carrier Block Island in 1945.

For more information about books from
Classic Warships Publishing,
please visit our website:

www.classicwarships.com